Seed of Sarah

Seed
OF
Sarah

MEMOIRS OF A SURVIVOR

Judith Magyar Isaacson

UNIVERSITY OF ILLINOIS PRESS
Urbana and Chicago

This book is printed on acid-free paper.

Portions of Chapter 5 appeared in an earlier version as "Seed of Sarah:
A Memoir" in *The Yale Review,* 73 (Spring 1984). Copyright 1984 by Judith
Magyar Isaacson.

Library of Congress Cataloging-in-Publication Data

Isaacson, Judith Magyar, 1925–
    Seed of Sarah : memoirs of a survivor / Judith Magyar Isaacson.
        p.   cm.
    Bibliography: p.
    Includes index.
    ISBN 0-252-01651-3
    1. Jews—Hungary—Kaposvár—Persecutions.   2. Holocaust, Jewish (1939–
1945—Hungary—Kaposvár—Personal narratives.   3. Isaacson, Judith Magyar,
1925–   .   4. Auschwitz (Poland : Concentration camp)   5. Kaposvár (Hungary)—Ethnic relations.   I. Title.
DS135.H92K375   1990
940.54'72'43094386—dc19   89-4737
                                                                      CIP

For our children
and
our children's
children

Aki él, az mind, mind örüljön—
All who live, rejoice, rejoice.
Endre Ady

Contents

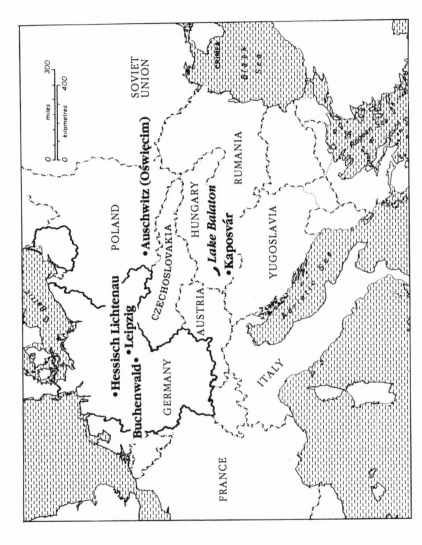

Map of Europe during World War II showing my travels.

PREFACE
How Can You Smile?
Brunswick, Maine • November 1976

In my teens, I planned to study literature at the Sorbonne, and while in Auschwitz I vowed to record my experiences in a book. I even dreamt of filming them in Hollywood. But after the war I had no more desire to write, and I hardly ever spoke of my former life, except to my children.

When I returned to school in my mid-thirties, I chose to study mathematics. It was my way of repressing the past—until events dictated otherwise.

• • •

In February 1973, my husband and I spent a vacation in Trinidad, farther than we'd ever been before, and on our way back, we decided to detour through Venezuela. In Caracas, we bumped into a couple of English-speaking boys lugging costumes, who explained that they were students at a Jewish day school on their way to a Purim festival.[1] They invited us to join them, and we found ourselves with a group of Spanish-speaking parents watching a biblical masquerade.

The costumes were easy to identify—the traditional Esthers, Hamans, and Mordecais were joined by various characters from the Old

---

1. Purim celebrates the Jews' victory over Syria as portrayed in the Old Testament's Book of Esther.

Testament: I recall an Abraham with a ram's horn and a David with a harp, a female slave of Egypt, and a lanky Moses with twin cardboard tablets on his back.

"Ike," I said, "whom do you think that girl represents, the one dancing with Moses."

"The one with chains? Why, she represents you, of course!"

"Oh, no!" I cried, my body pimpling with goose flesh. But of course Ike was right, the girl's dress was a striped imitation of our concentration camp outfit, her chains symbolic, and as she turned, I glimpsed her childish yellow star, fashioned of construction paper.

Ike noticed my shock and reached for my hand: "What's the matter? Don't you approve?"

"I find it disturbing."

• • •

All this came back to me some three years later, in November 1976, when a request came from Bowdoin College to give a talk. I was then Dean of Students at Bates College, and appearing at neighboring Bowdoin seemed routine enough. But someone had found out about my background, and I was asked to speak following a film on the Holocaust. I wanted to refuse, but could not. This proved fortunate: the powerful French documentary, *Night and Fog,* acted on me like a catalyst.

After the film, I dabbed the tears and mounted the podium with clenched fists. Our young host introduced me briefly: "Our speaker this evening: Judith Magyar Isaacson; Dean of Students at Bates College; Bowdoin alumna with an M.A. in mathematics; survivor of Auschwitz." How incongruous, I thought.

Rather than making a set speech, I suggested an informal discussion, and it was accepted warmly. Facing a college audience soon propelled me into my accustomed role, and despite the barrage of traumatic questions, I regained my cheerful dean's persona. Since I had just seen the film, memories I had long repressed suddenly came alive, and I answered each question with an episode—from Kaposvár, Auschwitz, Lichtenau, and Leipzig. To my surprise, I found I could relive the past without much anguish.

It was well past eleven when a pigtailed student stood up in the front row. "Dean Isaacson," she said, "may I ask you a *personal* question?" Her eyes, all pupils, were sad, her pitch belligerent. She was putting my deanly dignity to the test. "Ask anything you like," I told her, smiling but tense. "Must I answer?"

Laughter rewarded me from the jammed hall, but my pretty

questioner did not join in. "Dean," she probed, thrusting a bold chin, "how old were you in Auschwitz?"

"Nineteen—in 1944," I told her. "Now you can figure my age."

Laughter rippled, and scanning the raised hands, I smiled, relieved: "Next question, please."

But my youthful interrogator hadn't finished. Swinging back her braids with a shake of her head, she shuddered as she said: "Nineteen, like me . . . Dean Isaacson, were you raped in the camps?"

"Raped?" I blanched, reliving the panic. "Raped, you said? I'll tell you how I escaped it . . ." The packed hall receded into silence.

It was past midnight when I finished the tale. Among the people who grabbed my hand was a lanky, spectacled young man. "There's one more question I'd like to ask you before you leave," he caught me at the door. "After all you've been through, how can you smile? So freely? So often?"

"I smiled?" I gasped. "About Lichtenau and Auschwitz?"

"You did. Frequently."

"You may be right," I mumbled, apologetically. "Sorry, I don't know why . . . I don't know how . . . I must think about it. Yes, I'll certainly think about it."

That night I dreamt of Lichtenau, woke at five in the morning, sleepwalked to the typewriter and started to write.

I

THE HIDDEN CROWD
Kaposvár, Hungary • Spring 1938

KAPOSVÁR: a speck on some maps, a void on most. "Virágzó
Kaposvár—Blooming Kaposvár" perches in the hills beyond the
Danube, the dozing capital of Somogy county in southwest Hungary.
Kaposvár was my home, my universe.

Mother, father, and I lived on Kontrássy Street, on the second floor
of a two-story house, in four bright, spacious rooms. Our rented apartment spread above the *Somogy Journal,* and the daily rumble of the
printing press would be the only thing to shake the tranquility of our
lives.

On school days, the bathroom was always mine from seven to a
quarter past. Mother would wake me five minutes earlier, because I
liked to spend the time lying under my *dunyha*, a puffy down quilt. On
winter mornings, I needed those extra minutes just to gather courage
to get up.

I would strip to the waist in the unheated bathroom to give myself
a fast rubdown with icy water, watching steam rise from my shoulders.
At thirteen, I liked to linger at the mirror which reflected a new me,
with an elongated waist and two tiny jutting breasts. Then I would pull
on winter underwear and my school uniform, a pleated navy skirt and
a blouse styled like a hussar jacket. The Hungarian Ministry of Education had recently ordered all private schools to exchange their traditional sailor blouses for this national motif. Someone in government
must have had a fit of patriotism—in defiance of Hitler, I hoped.

"You can have the bathroom now," I would call, and my father
would come, humming a *csárdás*—a Hungarian dance tune. He would
halt his morning singing only to shave. With the razor dancing on his
cheeks, he would purse his lips and whistle instead.

Mother with me (July 3, 1926).

Mother, father, and I (1934).

My parents on their fifteenth anniversary (1938). Mother's velvet robe was sewn for her by my aunt Magda.

His gleaming white skin and brisk stride made him seem much younger than his thirty-eight years. His face was lean with a short, straight nose, which I admired, fearing that my own might someday acquire the slight Vágó bent that came to my mother's family in late adolescence. A Jewish nose—what a curse that would be! More than ever before, everyone aped the "Aryan" look, however senseless Hitler's designation might be.

On snowy mornings I would join my mother at the family-room window to watch the snow. "Esik a hó, a dal ma megered—Snow flakes descending, stove's hearth throbbing"—mother liked to quote the well-known line from Babits, the twentieth-century poet, whenever we woke to a snowy morning. Babits and Ady—the Hungarian Verlaine and Baudelaire—were our favorites; we both knew scores of their poems by heart.

I would answer her with a line from Shelley—in the Hungarian translation, of course: "Késhet a tavasz, ha már itt a tél?—If winter comes, can spring be far behind?"

The room would be fragrant with burning wood and fresh-baked rolls, brought from my grandfather Vágó's bakery by his young apprentice, who delivered them daily in a wicker pack-basket, as he did to scores of customers. Mother would step lightly toward our massive tile stove—the color of burnished copper—and stretch her arms to the purring, tall, rectangular solid as if it were a living thing. I liked her best in her ankle-length robe of black corduroy, patterned with miniature yellow roses that set off her wavy, seal-black hair.

Breakfast was always a croissant and an emperor's brioche, with fresh butter and my mother's homemade jam. I always drank cocoa and my parents had café-au-lait.

Punctually at 7:45 I would leave for school, only three blocks away on Eszterházy promenade, Kaposvár's only asphalt-paved street. Along the icy sidewalks two strips of snow hid the canna beds, two long, dirty *dunyhas*. Bare trees stood guard, trembling in the wind.

I attended the third form in the girls' *Gimnazium*—Somogy county's only preparatory school for the more-bookish daughters of the middle class, a nonsectarian school of eight forms, for ages ten to eighteen. Its three-story, grey stone structure was impressive, until one compared it to the boys' counterpart, which resembled a palace.

I always made it to school by five minutes to eight and would dash up to the second floor two steps at a time—my private game, a secret superstition, like dodging cracks in asphalt pavements.

•   •   •

One day, my race was suddenly interrupted by no less a personage than Dr. Ferenc Biczó (pronounced Bitzō), a professor of the upper forms, who was a colorful, controversial figure and a brilliant lecturer in Hungarian and Latin literature. He stood on the landing, a veritable statue of himself, one foot posed before the other, hands clasped behind his back in studied nonchalance. His open coat exposed a protruding vest bursting its buttons and the narrow slit of a pocket, which held a heavy gold watch and chain. He was a bachelor, whom several upper-form girls hoped to marry on graduation—despite his round paunch, bald pate, and forty-odd years.

Mesmerized by his august presence, I stopped, looked hesitantly, and for the first time saw at close range the ruddy cheeks, the gold-rimmed spectacles, and the fleshy nose with blue and crimson veins. A Mona Lisa smile, in a middle-aged, male edition, played furtively on his thin, purple lips. It was rumored in town that he liked his wine. The alcohol, it was said, gave him inspiration.

Dr. Biczó was something of a local legend in Kaposvár, a town given to culture almost as much as to gossip. My young aunt Magda Vágó, a great Biczó admirer, had prepared me to honor his exalted position long before I entered the gimnazium.

"Magyar," Dr. Biczó pronounced in a lordly cadence. He knew my name!

"Yes," I whispered. A biblical "Here am I!" would have better fitted my mood, for I felt as if I had been addressed by a divine presence.

"You are Magda Vágó's niece," he said. "Vágó, a young lady of talent." I barely nodded. My favorite aunt was eight years my senior; I was amazed that Biczó knew the connection.

"Please, Vágó—I mean Magyar—report to my office at ten o'clock recess." He continued his stately ascent without a word of explanation.

After this exalted command, I skipped the steps three at a time, my braids flying off at the sides. I paid only scant attention to the morning lectures, and, as soon as the bell rang for recess, I dashed to the third floor, the upper-form territory. But once there, I slowed down considerably, awed by the elongated torsos and round breasts parading up and down the corridor.

Biczó's study was off limits to all but his privileged. It took most of the courage I could muster to approach his inner sanctum. When I appeared at the open door, he glanced at me momentarily over his gold-rimmed spectacles, and then returned to his reading. His study was lined with books, arranged by subject, from floor to ceiling. A pale February sun washed the heavy oak desk and illuminated a small, exquisite oil painting on the far wall. Slowly, theatrically, he lifted his bald pate. "Hmm . . . Judit Magyar." I had the distinct impression that he enjoyed my amazement, and I gave a mute curtsy, just as mother had taught me: right tiptoe behind left foot, fingertips lifting the rim of the navy pleated skirt to the prescribed one centimeter.

Biczó leaned back in his chair, crossing his short arms over his stout chest. "Well, Magyar," he said, "I understand you recite poetry." He had heard! I nodded, feeling my face grow warm. Dr. Biczó closed the book ponderously as he added: "I understand that you won first prize in the lower-form competitions."

That gave me back my courage: "I did. With a poem by Ady."

"Ady, no less! Well, I've got something far less sophisticated for you." His thin lips dipped at the corners, then slowly eased into a smile. "How would you like to be the sole representative of the lower forms at our March Fifteenth Festival?"

March Fifteenth was the anniversary of the 1848 Hungarian revolution, and the yearly festival was the only public performance offered by our gimnazium. Everybody of importance came, from the mayor to the shopkeepers. Within the world of the lower forms, a solo performance at the festival was like winning the Nobel Prize. There was nothing higher to strive for.

"At the March Fifteenth Festival?" I gasped, hardly believing.

"Yes, at the festival," he smiled, and handed me a book opened to a lengthy poem. I blushed deeply, and Dr. Biczó chuckled. "Recess is nearly over," he said, "you'd better get back downstairs, Magyar."

Returning to class, I was as concerned about a costume as I was about the poem. I would have to appear in a national dress, hand made for a small fortune. I did not want to tax my parents with such an unnecessary expense. My best friend, Ilona Pogány, soon offered me hers, but it proved too short. Next day, I rushed up to the second floor during recess. Overcoming my shyness, I called at the door of the sixth form: "Does anybody have an outgrown Hungarian costume?"

Marika Erdős jumped up: "You're Judit Magyar, aren't you ?" I merely nodded. Everyone knew Marika; she was a celebrated upper-form scholar and performer. But I hardly expected her to know of me. "I hear you're to recite the lower-form poem at the festival," she said. "I did, three years ago, and I'm sure mother kept my costume. Let me see . . ." she sized me up with her eyes. "Oh, yes, it'll fit you fine!"

The next morning, Marika brought the dress to school. I was overjoyed. Costumes were generally paprika-red, sheet-white, and grass-green, resembling the Hungarian flags, but Marika's was unique. The vest and headdress were fashioned of crimson velvet, decorated with sparkling stones. Over the embroidered white silk skirt hung a miniature jade green apron—a work of art.

"I shall be wearing Marika Erdős's costume," I boasted to Dr. Biczó during our rehearsal, proud of the connection.

"Oh, Marika Erdős," Biczó beamed, "one of my top young scholars." Three years my senior, Marika was all I wanted to become: tall, sophisticated, dashing. The fact that she was not Jewish did not concern me, but the fact that she had fashionably full breasts did. I envied their soft bounce under her navy uniform. I expected to grow tall, and I strove to become dashing and sophisticated, but only God could bestow such breasts.

I learned my poem by heart and rehearsed it for hours each night. Unfortunately it was a patriotically contrived ode, trite and childish. "Don't exaggerate that awful rhythm," mother coached, "you're rocking me to sleep. Tone it down. And make your voice resonant: like silver bells in the wind." But camouflaging the rhymes and rhythm wasn't easy. Even while I practiced diligently, I couldn't help but laugh at the poem, so amateurish compared to an Ady or a Babits. I complained to my aunt Magda. "It smacks of the principal," she jeered with the patronizing air of the recently graduated. "I'm sure Dr. Biczó didn't choose it." But as the weeks passed, the poem grew on me, and as I declaimed to mother, I waxed so emotional that tears collected on my lashes. Hadn't my great-grandfather Weiss volunteered in the revolution? Hadn't my father and my paternal uncles fought in the World War? Secretly, I prayed for another upheaval and the chance to risk my own life for my country.

A few days before the festival, Dr. Biczó listened to me recite the poem in its entirety. He nodded his bald head with satisfaction: "Just think what you could do with a great poet like Ady."

The next day, March 13, 1938, which turned out to be a day of historical significance, raced by like any other for me. School in the morning, our main meal at noon. After a dish of veal stew and several walnut-filled *palacsintas*—Hungarian crêpes—my parents lay down on the divan for their siesta, and I was off for a private lesson in French shared by Ilona. Afterwards, we played in her yard.

In the evening, I had supper, poem rehearsal, and homework.

By parental edict, bedtime came punctually. I slept on the studio couch in the family room, and had already crept under my *dunyha* when father turned on the forbidden voice of BBC from London, broadcasting in German. Our radio set was a novel gadget, its unnatural voice a shocking intrusion. But I knew how to block it out.

Mother was listening to the news while knitting by our copper-colored stove; her elegant, long fingers whirled, making me pleasantly drowsy. Father knelt in front of the radio, as if in prayer, on the elaborate little Persian rug mother had made for his birthday, last April. His fingers turned the dials: BBC was difficult to get. His back was to me, slim and supple under his herringbone coat, and his light brown hair was close-clipped where it met the neck—the short, powerful neck I loved. Secure and serene, I was drifting off to sleep when a male voice announced in German: "This is BBC . . . Hitler's armies occupied Austria today . . . At this very moment, Jewish women are on their hands and knees mopping up Vienna's major promenades . . ." I sat up, terrified. Hungary would be next on Hitler's route. And we were so near . . . Will my mother be mopping up Kaposvár's Fő Ucca[1] (Main Street)? I already saw her, slumped on her hands and knees, her lovely hands blue from the icy rags and her black wool coat dragging in horse dung.

As soon as father shut off the radio, I confronted him with "Will Hitler try to take over Hungary too, Papa?"

Father bit his lower lip. "I hope not . . ."

"What if he decides to gobble us up?" I anguished. "Would our army repel him?"

My father was a reserve officer, and I expected total reassurance. But he only muttered as if to himself, "They would, if they could." Seeing my fright, he embraced me. "Don't fret, Jutka (pronounced Yutka). We'll stop them before they cross that border! Go to sleep now; there is school tomorrow."

At breakfast, my parents spoke only of the Germans, of Hitler and Vienna. They turned on Radio Budapest, the government mouthpiece. Just the day before, its tone seemed almost impartial, but now it parroted Berlin: "the victorious German armies . . . the Jewish women in their ill-gotten jewelry . . ."

"My God, my God," mother frowned, "and Austria was occupied only yesterday! Will Horthy[2] sell out completely? I don't trust him, Jani. Do you?"

I was aghast. How could my mother speak of our governor Horthy disrespectfully? Father shook his head and waved toward the closed door to whisper: "Watch out! What if Mari is listening?" We had a maid like most middle-class families, since wages were minimal and housework arduous, but our village maid, Mari, was hardly a Nazi spy. How nervous my parents must be, I thought, alarmed.

---

1. Ucca is the spelling we used. It has since been changed to Utca.
2. Miklos Horthy, whom we called *kormanyzó* 'governor', had headed the government since November 1920, when he was appointed "temporary" regent.

"What about Jutka's recital?" mother burst out. "A Jewish girl can't very well appear as a symbol of Hungarian womanhood now."

Father's blue-grey eyes grew dim behind the glasses, "I guess you'd better resign, Szivecském—my little heart—before they tell you to. Go and see Dr. Biczó about it first thing this morning."

At quarter to eight, I was in Dr. Biczó's study. He did not seem at all surprised to see me. Did he know I was Jewish? Yes, he did, but it did not matter; this was Hungary, not Austria. Shouldn't I resign my role just the same? Absolutely not, he said. "This is a private institution of classical learning, not some public school."

"Yes," I murmured, "but will the principal allow it?"

Biczó jumped from his chair to pace the room. "He'd better allow it, if he wants his festival," Dr. Biczó waved me off, kindly but firmly.

If Easter was for Christians and Passover for Jews, March Fifteenth was a holiday for all Hungarians. We children always wore spring coats and white knee socks for the first time, no matter how icy the weather. It was the only way to display the ribboned corsages, red, white, and green, like a bouquet of spring flowers. As I stepped onto Kontrássy Street, breathing the sunlit, purified air, I hummed one patriotic song after another. The scare I had suffered two days before had vanished. Vienna seemed far away, and Hitler's armies safely beyond the borders.

Kontrássy Street was celebrating with me: the two-storied houses were on parade, joyfully waving their tricolored flags. Corsaged and light-footed, I, too, was part of the holiday. But carefree as I might have seemed, my child's instincts feared doom; even as I skipped and hummed my way to school, my feet automatically leaped over each crack in the pavement.

Today, our classes were celebrations, and the whole day was spent with history, poetry, and song. In the evening I arrived at school in Marika's splendid costume, jumping with excitement. Among the participants, I was the only child. Our art instructor made up my face with the concentration of a true artist. She held me at arm's length: "You look lovely, Magyar: the picture of a little *Hungarian* girl." She thinks I don't look Jewish, I figured, and skipped off, foolishly taking it for a compliment.

My poem was second in the program. All through the Bartók-Kodály choirs, I trembled behind the heavy, plush curtains, waiting for Dr. Biczó's cue. At the stroke of his plump finger, I parted the crimson drapes and stepped on stage. Mother had warned me of this terrifying moment: "Just pretend that all those heads are cabbages." But unfortunately there were no heads for me to see. Only darkness, threatening darkness. Under the dazzling light, I stood isolated, vulnerable. I curtsied, lifting the embroidered silk skirt with two fingers, and heard my voice choke up as I announced the title and author. Breathlessly, childishly, I began:

> Magyar lányok, tudjátok-e
> Micsoda nap van ma?
> A magyar nép dicsőségét
> E nagy naptól kapta.

> Hungarian girls, say,
> What day is today?
> *Magyar* people's glory
> Stems from this day.

"Shut up, Jewess!" a belligerent voice thundered from the void. Coarse shouts startled me from terribly near: "Dirty Jew!" "Away with the Kike!" Shrill, mocking whistles sprang up from all directions, hissing their hatred and spite. I shivered, terrified. Our friendly auditorium, where I had so often played and exercised, was transformed into an enemy den. Unseeing, I faced a nightmare. My knees shook above the white knee socks and my teeth chattered audibly. All my instincts propelled me backstage. But I would not give in.

I took a deep breath and dug my nails deep into my palms. My eyes had become accustomed to the spotlights, and I forced them to stare into the void. I gave another curtsy, this time low, unhurried, formal—just as I had learned in folk dance. Proud of my newfound courage, I smiled involuntarily.

Applause sprang from the dark hall, first sporadically, then solidly from all directions. Here and there, a mocking whistle soared above the clapping, but no one shouted anymore.

I decided to recite my poem from the start:

> Hungarian girls, say
> What day is today?

My voice surprised me. It was fuller, stronger than before, almost adult. The large hall echoed it encouragingly, and there were no interruptions until the final din of applause. One more curtsy, and I backed offstage, exhausted but exhilarated.

"Well done," smiled Dr. Biczó, and I ran to change into my navy dress uniform with the tricolor corsage.

It was with some trepidation that I went to Dr. Biczó's study the next morning to return the book containing my poem. What would he say about the Nazi interference? Could he possibly understand how terrifying it had been?

He received me kindly, "Excellent performance! Your voice is well suited to a large auditorium." Not a word about the demonstrators.

"The whistles . . ." I mumbled.

"Oh, yes!" he interrupted. "Some lunatic fringe, no doubt. Do you know, Magyar, how many *Nyilasok*—Arrowcross[3]—there are in all of Kaposvár? No more than a hundred, surely. In a population of thirty-five thousand." He rapped his pencil against the desk for emphasis. "They pose no danger. I hope they did not frighten you."

"Oh, no . . ." I hung my head.

"Have you ever read Plato, Judit Magyar?"

I hardly knew who Plato was. "We haven't had him, professor, sir."

Dr. Biczó stepped to the nearest bookshelf and slowly, with great formality, extracted a thin, worn volume and handed it to me. "You may take it home, Magyar, but please, be careful. I don't make a habit of lending my books to students. Note the dialogue *Gorgias,* and remember, Magyar, what Socrates teaches us: 'It is better to suffer an injustice than to commit one.' "

I held the frayed book as if in prayer. "Thank you, professor, sir," I curtsied. Down in the courtyard, a willful March wind bent the shivering poplars. I watched through Dr. Biczó's window as one of the young trees bowed humbly to the ground and stood upright again.

---

3. The Hungarian Nazis' emblem was an arrowed cross, in lieu of the swastika.

2
GRANDFATHER ESCAPES
Kaposvár, Hungary • December 1938

> The expansion of the Jews is as detrimental to the nation as it is dangerous. We must take steps to defend ourselves against their propagation. Their relegation to the background is a national duty.
>
> (Preamble, First Jewish Law, lex XV, ex 1938—Hungary)

AFTER the occupation of Austria on March 13, 1938, the condition of Hungarian Jews deteriorated daily. In May, discrimination was sanctioned by the First Jewish Law, causing economic hardships. In September, Jewish students lost their scholarships, and new Nazi textbooks changed history overnight: from Roman times to the present, the Jews emerged as villains. Most of our professors ignored the new politics; Aladár Kőváry, my history teacher, was the only exception. He suddenly emerged as an avowed antisemite, and he seemed to get a perverse enjoyment out of spouting obscenities at the Jewish girls.

Kőváry towered on his podium, a bony giant with a small head, wiry eyebrows, and piercing eyes. He flapped his arms like a bird of prey and stretched his long neck as far as it would go. Behind his back we called him *Csutka*—Adam's Apple; in class, we snickered at the oversized protrusion, which bobbed up and down like a yo-yo.

Mr. Kőváry neither assigned papers nor gave any written exams; our grades depended solely on oral presentation. Even the best students worried about grades; with a single "B" chances of acceptance at university would become precarious. Wickedly, he chose Jewish girls to recite the most antisemitic passages. But soon we each found our defensive tactics. I, for instance, would introduce each paragraph with: "According to the *latest* historical hypotheses . . ."

Évi Kárpáti was far more creative. She rose with a defiant shake of her head to declaim: "In the Middle Ages, all the usurers were . . . *Germans!*" Then she quickly corrected herself: "Sorry, I meant Jews." At other times, she recited like a little dramatic actress: "The *holy* heroes of the *holy* wars staged *holy* pogroms."

She got away with it because she was so popular and so comic. Soon Kőváry ignored the rest of us, having found an easy victim in Böde Winternitz, a gawky girl who sat in the back row.

"Come on Winternitz!" Adam's Apple thundered. "Don't omit anything! Surely, those Jews deserved what they got! Now, give us the reasons, you red-faced monkey!"

I turned back in my seat. So did thirty-eight other navy-clad girls. What would Böde say? Her face turned crimson and her dark eyes pleaded. "The Middle Ages . . ." she stuttered. "The Jews . . . The moneylenders . . ."

"Cow's udder between bull's horns!" Kőváry bellowed. Thirty-nine uniformed young ladies dipped pens into inkwells and copied "Cow's udder between bull's horns" into their notebooks. We loved to spread Kőváry's novel vulgarities during recess. Böde clutched her desk and closed her eyes; two tears slid down her inflamed cheeks. But her tormentor hadn't finished. "Tell me, you offspring of blushing idiots, where did those worthless Jews come from? Stay mum another minute and I'll flunk you out of here without another chance. One less Jewish intellectual to worry about! Go, hide yourself in your father's grocery shop!"

That did it. Böde hated helping in her father's store. Burly peasants filled it on market days, and she was much too shy to take their good-natured jocosities. Quickly, she quoted from our textbook: "During the Middle Ages, the Jews infiltrated Hungary, mostly from Poland, Galicia, and Rumania . . ." She hesitated, emitted a half-choked sob, then switched to the text we had three years previously: "But the Israelites in western Hungary are descendants of the Kazars!" We Jews of Somogy county prided ourselves on our "Aryan" ancestry: prejudice is contagious, and imperceptibly we had absorbed the media's bias. In self-irony, we often paraphrased Hitler's slogan "Heraus mit den Juden!—Out with the Jews!" to "Heraus mit uns!—Out with us!"

"You improvising donkey with an elephant's trunk!" Kőváry sputtered. A shocked sigh sprang from the class. This was just too much—even from Adam's Apple.

Ági Toronyi stuck up both hands, waving them insistently. The daughter of a prominent gentile doctor, she would not be ignored. "Toronyi," Kőváry nodded.

Ági took her time, for the stage was clearly hers. With an exaggerated poise, she smoothed down her pleated skirt and threw back her head. Instead of her boyish voice, she sounded resonant and calm, almost grown-up. "Professor, sir, we learned about the Kazars in first form. They were a nomad tribe who adopted Judaism before they joined the Magyars in the occupation of present-day Hungary."

"Who is teaching whom?" Kőváry bellowed. "Jewish horsemen! Bahhh! Legends of the past. The Kazars are gone. Wiped out! There isn't any mention of them in your textbook."

Évi Kárpáti couldn't take it anymore: her right arm waving like a flag, she cried out passionately: "They weren't lost for a *thousand* years! We still had them in first form!"

There was a peal of appreciative laughter, underscored by the bells for recess. Kőváry grabbed his book and left the room, followed by a surge of my classmates.

Squirming my way through the crowd, I rushed upstairs, and caught a fifth former by the door: "Guess what's Kőváry's latest? 'Cow's udder between bull's horns!' Gross, isn't it?" As she repeated it to her friends, I grinned, rewarded. "Have you seen Pogány?" I asked.

"She's still inside."

I barged into the fifth-form classroom to look for Ilona Pogány, my best friend ever since I could remember. Our mothers had been closest friends since adolescence, and it seemed to me that Ilona and my aunt Magda were given to me in lieu of sisters.

I now found Ilona surrounded by her classmates, the shortest and blondest among them. As always, she had an air of calm about her; I kept Kőváry's obscenity to myself. We touched fingertips, a greeting we had. "What's up, Jutka?"

"It's about Winternitz," I whispered.

Böde and Ilona lived across the street from each other—the Pogánys in the best house on Castle Street, the Winternitzes in a modest home hugging their grocery. There were other differences: the Pogánys were more assimilated, even the name Pogány, meaning pagan, was an assertion of Kazar ancestry, a patriotic name like Magyar or Kárpáti.

"You've got to talk to Böde," I told Ilona as we started our two-by-two march along the corridor, and quickly I related the incident.

"Poor Böde," Ilona shook her head, "one minute shy, next minute defiant. She's being oversensitive again."

"How can you say that?" I said, indignant. "Adam's Apple is sure to flunk her. He's out for a victim."

"I don't believe it."

'He's a well-known Nazi," I protested.

"That may be true, Jutka," Ilona shook her head, "but he hasn't flunked her yet. Don't be unfair."

"You're being naive," I bristled. "Stop reading Dostoyevski."

"And you stop telling me that 'It is better to suffer an injustice than to commit one.' "

"All right, no more Socrates," I said, as the bells rang. It was impossible to get her angry.

Life at our school continued unchanged, but by December Parliament was debating the Second Jewish Law, and my parents were increasingly nervous.

Mother paled when father came home early on a Friday afternoon. "Jani, what happened?" she cried, running to the door. Father looked ill, stooped and trembling. "Father died!" he blurted. "A blood clot—it rushed to his heart."

We hurried to his parents' home. The gate was unlocked, the door ajar. We rushed upstairs and into the living room. My tiny grandmother Klein paced the floors in her high-heeled shoes, grey hair disheveled, meager bun askew. She used to be my playmate when I was a child, and I wanted to give her a big hug as I used to do. But I was frozen. Grandfather's body rested on the divan by the far wall, reminding me of ghost stories. Father tiptoed over and knelt by the corpse as if his father were asleep.

The room reassured me with its familiar smells of plants and cigar smoke. The polished tables bore grandmother's Herend figurines in harmony with grandfather's sterling silver cigar boxes and ashtrays: gifts from former pupils to their teacher and principal. The two giant chrysanthemums I had brought for grandfather's seventy-sixth birthday beckoned to me encouragingly from the windowsill.

There was only one sign of the recent heart attack: grandfather's favorite chair had tipped sideways, the four legs jarring the cluttered harmony of the room.

Moving out of my trance, I set the chair upright. On the table, a handsome volume of Goethe's collected poems lay open to a sonnet. Grandfather and I had been reading German together for several years now, and I now wondered whether he had chosen this sonnet for our next lesson. It isn't the sort of message O'papa would pick for me—I

My paternal grandparents, Sidonia and Simon Klein (1939).

thought, as I read Goethe's *Wanderers Nachtlied*. Perhaps he chose it for himself: "Warte nur, balde, ruhest du auch—Wait, soon, you too will rest."

Cautiously, I took a small step toward the sofa, where grandfather lay. Only his necktie had been loosened; his suit-jacket was buttoned, his black shoes gleaming. "Come, Jutka, don't be afraid," father beckoned to me. Tense and trembling, I stepped over. I looked at the bald crown, wisps of silver hair, chiseled nose with bronze hussar mustache, closed eyes defenseless without the glasses. Grandfather's face was at rest.

Along the side of the sofa, grandfather's left hand hung rigid and pallid—his single-jointed little finger standing apart in a proud stance I loved. Next to it, a signet ring. Grandmother knelt down and removed it from the dead hand. "Father would want you to have it, Jani," she whispered, as she slipped it next to my father's own single-jointed little finger. "You were his favorite son." Father's hand now became a replica of grandfather's. Would my own son inherit that gold signet ring, that rebellious little finger?

Next day was Sabbath, so the funeral was set for Sunday. In the morning, during a blizzard, father, mother, and I went to my grandparents' house, wearing black arm bands. As we passed the great Romanesque Catholic church, we watched an exceptional multitude battle the storm from all directions, fleeing through its vaulted doors.

"It's Christmas," I exclaimed, "Christmas and Sunday! It would happen only once every seven years."

"No gentile will come to the funeral," mother softly said, linking her arm into father's. "Don't be disappointed, Jani."

"They'll come," father protested. "Remember, darling, 'Peace on earth, good will toward men.' It includes Jews."

Grandfather's pine coffin lay on the living room floor, the lid loosely nailed—an orthodox touch in a Neologue[1] home. It made me recall my Hebrew lessons with a shiver: "The coffin must be left in readiness for the coming of the Messiah." Father stepped to it as soon as we entered; small clumps of snow slipped from his coat and melted into the red Torontal carpet.

The apartment was crowded: black-clad people with bleached faces clustered around the dull coffin, stark against a somber background. Grandmother's mirrors and paintings were all draped over with white linen bedsheets. "Why has Nana covered the pictures?" I asked

---

1. Neologue, the dominant Jewish religion in Western Hungary, was similar to American conservative Judaism.

mother in a whisper. I knew that in a house of mourning, only the mirrors had to be hidden.

"I don't know," she shook her head, but her smile belied her. Then I remembered my favorite oil, a stylized village scene with small boys competing to see who could pee the farthest. Grandmother had been objecting to the picture ever since the day grandfather bought it. She must have thought it especially shameful in a house of mourning.

Grandmother was silently weeping on the sofa, next to Ica (pronounced Etza), her only daughter. My aunt was barely recognizable, her miniature form swathed in black and her brilliant bronze hair—the color of grandfather's mustache—hidden under a black hat and veil. Familiar freckles dotted her dainty white nose. Childless and provincial, Ica let herself be exploited by her boss, a bank president, and was subservient to her husband, Zoltán Gyenes, an overbearing teacher. She relaxed only with her parents.

"Don't cry, Mama, don't cry, my dear," Ica whispered. But behind her convex glasses, swollen, red veins stood out, magnified. Mother and daughter talked quietly side by side on the sofa, where only yesterday grandfather's corpse had lain. They were like twin rag dolls, their tiny black shoes barely touching the floor. The rest of the women had joined the children in the next room. My father and two of his brothers gathered around the green-clad table to talk. The uncles had traveled quite a distance: Laci Klein from Budapest, Józsi Magyar from east of the Danube. Only Feri, the American, was missing. The three men had much to say to each other. How could they chat in the presence of that coffin? I shuddered and backed into a corner.

"Well, we are burying the last of the Kleins," Uncle Laci announced. Laci was the sole dark-haired one, with sentimental eyes and a defiant chin. The only one who still clung to the family name, Klein. He had been a prisoner of war when the rest of the family changed their name to Magyar, and by the time he got back during the counterrevolution of 1919, the climate was so antisemitic Laci felt disenchanted.

Father raised his head. "Are you going to change your name to Magyar then?"

Laci's mouth curled down at the corners. "No way!" he cried out.

"Shhh," Józsi, the primary-school teacher, whispered, index finger to his mouth as he gestured toward the coffin.

I looked gratefully at homely Uncle Józsi, the archconservative. For the first time in my life, I found myself on his side. It was said that my grandmother was sick when she was pregnant with him; certainly

Józsi inherited all the family characteristics, but a bit distorted, symbolized by an ugly mole next to his mouth.

My father, though the youngest of the brothers, wasn't accustomed to heeding them. "Why shouldn't the four of us brothers have the same name?" he argued.

"Too late for that," Laci shook his head. "It's ironic enough that Feri should still be called 'Hungarian' in America."

"I had a letter from Feri just the other day," Father remembered. "He's about to lose his job at Marquette University. Apparently American youth are revolting against Hitler, and no one is taking German literature anymore—as if Thomas Mann, Goethe, or the Jew Heine were to blame for Nazism!"

"Poor Feri," Józsi muttered. "Father was so proud of him, his eldest, a professor in America. And he can't even make it home for the funeral!" Józsi pulled out the black-bordered handkerchief that his ever-doting wife had provided for him, wiped his eyes, and blew his nose—a bit too loudly, as was his custom.

"I don't understand, Laci," father put a hand on his arm: "Why do you change your name at all?"

"To keep my job. I've already arranged for a false certificate, listing me as a Christian."[2]

Józsi jumped up and grabbed his brother by the arm: "Laci! It's dangerous! It's sacrilegious! What would father say?"

"Father is dead," Laci said, hiding his face in his hands.

Józsi wiped his eyes with his black-edged handkerchief as he stepped to the window. "This storm won't let up. No one will come to the funeral."

Laci put a powerful arm about his brother's puny shoulders: "The Jews will come regardless, Józsi, and none of the gentiles will show up in any case. Not in these times."

"They will," said father. "You'll see!" My father and grandfather always expected people to act nobly—and people often did, out of respect for them.

In the afternoon, the funeral procession consisted of family only, our horse-drawn sleighs following the elaborate hearse on its silent runners. The Christmasy shop windows were draped in red velvet on the inside, white snow on the outside. No passersby. The horses panted, straining up the steep hill along upper Fő Ucca, and we covered our faces against the stinging spray.

---

2. In anticipation of the Second Jewish Law, which was about to become enacted.

"Perhaps Józsi was right," father mumbled into his black woolen scarf. "No gentile would want to climb three kilometers in this storm on a Christmas Sunday."

A throng had gathered at the heavy iron gates, waiting for our procession. The Hebrew congregation showed up en masse: people home for Christmas vacation, including my favorite uncle, Dezső Vágó from Budapest, who was waving to me discreetly. Gentiles came too, grandfather's chess partners, former pupils, and colleagues. Just as we dismounted, another set of sleighs pulled up: Mayor Kaposvári, followed by city officials, school principals, and priests—a sizable contingent of Kaposvár's all-Christian dignitaries.

"Look at this!" Uncle Laci gasped. "This town is not as antisemitic as I thought."

All through the funeral—the first one I had attended—I grieved for my grandfather, awed by the sonorous chants, desperate over the thud of frozen earth pounding on his lowered coffin—but I could not help watching the proceedings as if witnessing history.

Our rabbi, Dr. Hercog, was obviously touched by so fine an assembly. A proclaimed anti-Zionist and—like my grandfather—a staunch and eloquent Hungarian patriot, he took advantage of this impressive audience to deliver a timely sermon.

Instead of the rabbinical white garb I remembered from Yom Kippur, Rabbi Hercog wore a mantle fashioned of snow. The slight man I knew had vanished. A prophet towered before me, preaching from a swirling cloud. Over my grandfather's open grave, in the whipping storm, he gave an impassioned speech on the patriotism of Hungarian Jewry. He omitted nothing, from the Kazars to the heroes of the last war: "Simon Klein, this proud descendant of the Kazars . . . this devout Hungarian pedagogue . . . a refugée from Czech atrocities . . . gladly did he send his four sons to fight for our country . . ."

All about me, the crowd stood blanketed in snow. I searched the silent faces. What did the gentiles make of this? Did they question the injustice of the Jewish law, as our anxious rabbi so clearly intended? Or were they simply eager to be done, to get home from the storm?

In the ancient cemetery, the snow-clad gravestones lined up in a frozen replica of our own assembly. Rabbi Hercog seemed to address the dead as well as the living as he swept in the white scene with his white-robed arms: "This devout Israelite, this exemplary Hungarian, whose ancestors lived and died on this soil for a *thousand* years . . . And now, let us all pray together: 'Oh, Lord, who reignest on high, shelter under thy divine wings the soul of the departed . . .'"

The Second Jewish Law was passed the week after grandfather's funeral. During the month that followed, my father, hardly a pious Jew, suddenly adhered to all the memorial customs. He even abstained from shaving for the prescribed thirty days as if we were orthodox. In the mornings, he no longer sang or whistled, and our days now started with a stark remembrance of the dead.

Eventually, the formal signs of mourning were shed: the prayers, the black clothes, and the beard. My father resumed his daily shaving—without whistling.

Father seemed changed in other ways, too. One of his strongest links to Hungary was gone, and he focused all his hopes on a proposed move to America. He rushed out a letter to his favorite brother, Professor Francis Magyar, asking for emigration papers.

3
FOUR YEARS
Kaposvár, Hungary · 1939–1943

THE year 1939 started with a jolt: in January, my uncle Feri sent us three affidavits. His letter was contradictory: on the one hand, he promised to finance my college education; on the other, he discouraged us from coming altogether, making several references to the Depression. "Be prepared to work as a dishwasher, Jani," he warned, "there are no decent jobs to be had."

"A dishwasher!" mother cried. "You don't even know how to rinse a glass."

"Feri is a fool when it comes to business," father grumbled. "And to complain that his new teaching job isn't secure. My God! Who's secure nowadays?"

"You're being unfair, darling," mother soothed. "He promised to send Jutka to college. Wasn't that decent of him?"

"True," father allowed, encircling an arm about my shoulders. "Just think of it, Jutka. No *numerus clausus* in America."

Numerus clausus was a quota system established in 1920—the sole antisemitic measure of pre-Nazi Hungary—that held the Jewish university population at 6 percent.[1] It had barred my aunt Magda and my Vágó uncles from attending, including Dezső, the most talented mathematician the boys' gimnazium had ever prepared. Grades weren't enough for Jews to be admitted; you needed *protekció*—connections.

"I'm not worried about the *numerus clausus*, Papa," I protested. "There'll be a liberal regime long before I'm eighteen. You said so your-

---

1. Jews constituted approximately 6 percent of the Hungarian population in 1920, the year the ratio was set.

self." And I added, offended: "You're forgetting something: I want to become a professor of Hungarian literature—like Dr. Biczó."

"Why not study English literature?" he smiled. "Or better yet, return to your old dream, architecture. That's the profession!" I was amazed; father had never held—and could never hold—such ambitions for me in Hungary.

Grandmother Klein accepted our planned departure with resignation, but mother's family was incredulous. "America!" mourned grandmother Vágó. "Dear God, you won't be here for Magda's wedding."

"Mama is right," mother declared during supper. "We can't leave until Magda's married. She's like another daughter to me."

"Magda's only twenty-two," father protested. "And nobody's thinking of marriage these days."

"But what's the hurry?" mother objected. "There's no danger yet."

"Hitler means war," father returned. "I've got to get you out."

"Hitler won't last," I interrupted. "Everyone says so."

"Everyone's blind," father retorted in rare anger.

Our dining table was often cluttered with his collection of maps and ship schedules, and we all started English lessons. My uncle Dezső sent me a hand-cranked gramaphone with a set of language records for my fourteenth birthday. "If you must abandon me for the U.S.A., Jutka," he wrote, "I don't want you to be an ignoramus there."

Father had arranged a day off from work to take the *filléres*—penny train—to the capital. He came back, furious: "The Americans are deaf and dumb to the crisis: they make no concessions for Jews. Hungarians are on a five-year waiting list. Five years, with Hitler at the door!"

"But you're on the Czech quota, Jani," mother interjected.

"That's true," he fumed. "Ironic, isn't it?" Father's birthplace was annexed to Czechoslovakia right after the war, and being patriotic Hungarians, he and his family fled from it to Kaposvár.

"But why should Czechs be better than Hungarians?" I sputtered.

"Why are gentiles better than Jews?" said father. "Trouble is, we're on the wrong side again."

"You're not, Jani," mother reminded him. "Go, darling. You'll establish an existence for us. Jutka and I will be all right. Wars are more threatening to men."

"Not this war," father shook his head. "This war'll be different." He closed the door, and added in a whisper. "You'll come with me on a visitor's visa and stay, illegally."

"You can't mean it, Jani," mother gasped. "They'll put us all into jail! Your father would turn in his grave."

"Papa asked Feri to send us affidavits even before I did."

"Jani, you never told me." Mother wandered about the room, caressing a table, a chair, a pillow she had embroidered herself. "Can we take all this with us, Jani? Can we?"

"I don't know, darling," father sighed, sinking on a chair. "I just don't know."

In mid-February, father showed me the leading article in the *Somogy Journal*. The day before, on February 15, 1939, Premier Béla Imrédy had called a special meeting of Parliament to announce his resignation. He revealed to the shocked assembly that his ancestry had been part Jewish.

"Serves him right!" father chuckled.

Count Pál Teleki took over as prime minister, the same Count Teleki who had previously stated: "The majority of Hungarian Jewry is completely assimilated . . . From the racial point of view, Hungarian Jews are no longer Jews, but Magyars." Despite Teleki's convictions, the Second Jewish Law was declared on May 1. A Christian counted as a Jew if two of his grandparents were born Jewish. In our circles, the Second Jewish Law caused many friends and relatives to lose their jobs. Father stayed on, but with reduced salary.

Because of the Second Jewish Law, which involved everyone who did not have three Aryan grandparents, my uncle Laci Klein, who had already changed his name to Simon, now lived under a third, fake name, in order to keep his accountant's position.

"Good God, Laci," father exclaimed when his brother stepped off the train on a visit. "You look ill. What's the matter?"

"I can't sleep nights," Laci groaned as we walked toward grandmother Klein's apartment. He stopped for a minute to show us his false papers: "See? István Kovács, Protestant. I borrowed the identity of a dead man, but I might be imprisoned for it. Sorry," he added, waving at me, "I didn't mean to upset the child."

That summer, as my father intensified his plans for emigration, I grew painfully absentminded. I lost books, handkerchiefs, keys. I even locked myself out several times. "What's the matter with you, Jutka?" father scolded me on a sultry evening in August. "Now, you keep turning off the lights. We're trying to read." Five minutes later, I turned off the lights again. Am I sick? I wondered. Is it my period? It had been unusually painful. Or was I losing my mind? I must forget about Hitler and emigration. School will soon start, and my life will be normal.

On the first of September 1939, I was happily binding my fifth-form books into regulation navy paper when Radio Budapest announced the outbreak of World War II. Father leaped to the radio.

"Quick!" he cried. "Check on the doors. I've got to get London." Soon, BBC's familiar voice read the declaration of war between Germany and England. "We must leave for America sooner than I expected," father murmured.

"But Papa!" I cried. "I'm just starting fifth form. With Dr. Biczó."

"I'm sorry, Cica (pronounced Tzetza—Kitten)" father hugged me as he adjusted the volume. "It can't be helped." London's forbidden voice crackled in our cozy room, reporting ships mined on the Atlantic.

"It's too late, Jani," sighed mother. "Surely, you wouldn't put Jutka on a ship to be mined."

"I'd take that risk, rather than waiting around for Hitler," father murmured. But mother paid my tuition "just in case," and a week later I started fifth form. The weaker students had all dropped out: some thirty young ladies from the county of Somogy ascended to the exalted second floor of the girls' gimnazium at Kaposvár to be imbued with culture. No more Mr. Kőváry. No more mediocre teachers. I joined the prestigious literary club and promptly won second prize in the poetry-reciting contest, with a famous poem by Endre Ady: *Imádság Háboru Után*—Prayer after War.

At home, father was preparing a list for our rucksacks. "I'm afraid we'll have to lug everything across the border," he told mother. "There is no way to ship things anymore." Before my parents could sell the furniture, the army stepped in. Hungary was not at war yet when, on a bright September day, the mailman rang the bell, interrupting our dinner. He handed father a registered envelope: his army induction papers. Father crumpled our ship's schedule into the stove: "I won't be a deserter." He had received his military training during World War I, and was now assigned to one of the newly formed Jewish labor service units as a reserve officer. He bid us good-bye in his fancy dress uniform complete with insignia and a sword at his side, but on his left sleeve he wore the Jews' canary yellow arm band.

My Vágó uncles had been too young to serve during World War I; if called to the army reserves now, they'd be low-class laborers. There was no precedent for this. Traditionally, middle-class sons attended school until age eighteen and automatically qualified for officer's training.

Early in October, father sent us a snapshot: next to him stood a handsome young ensign, smiling into the lens. "Take a good look at him, Jutka," wrote father. "Someday, I hope to introduce him to you."

"What's Papa up to?" I complained.

"Let him dream, poor fellow," said mother. "Let him dream."

A few weeks later, I tucked the ensign's photo into a drawer, hav-

World War I (1918). Left to right: My father at age eighteen with my grandfather and my uncle Feri.

Father in his fancy officer's uniform (1941). Taken at the Jewish labor service camp in Salánk. Father is on the right.

Rowing on Lake Balaton (1939). Left to right: Father, Ilona Pogány's aunt, myself, Ilona, Anti Székely. (Of the group, I was the only one to survive the Holocaust.)

A bicycle excursion (1939). Anti Székely and I stand at the extreme left, Ilona Pogány at the extreme right. Zsuzsi Schwarzenberg faces the camera, her father is just barely visible, talking to Zsuzsi's boyfriend—who survived, like me.

ing acquired my first boyfriend, Anti Székely, a sophisticated youth of fifteen. Of course, we were not permitted to walk on the street together—it was against school rules. Instead, he came to our house to teach me to draw in charcoal and he serenaded me on his violin. But my love for him stayed childish and platonic, to his disappointment.

Mother held father's position at Hónig & Weinberger, the Pogány's prestigious wholesale grocery firm, until father's discharge in December. She acted as head bookkeeper but not as a manager, leaving all those responsibilities to her best friend, Jolán Pogány, whose gentle husband, Bandi, a pharmacist by training, did not pretend to business acumen.

• • •

Father had just recently come home when Dr. Biczó gave us a novel assignment. "Write me a list of all things white," he challenged. "Unshackle your imaginations." I came up with a poem. I remember one line only: "Papám halántéka az idén fehér lett—My Papa's temples whitened this year." Dr. Biczó called on me to read the long poem aloud to class, he then bestowed on me his highest honor. "Magyar," he pronounced, "from henceforth, you may carry my books." And so it was that I joined Dr. Biczó's harem, so called by the envious. We were a handsome lot, as I recall. Had Dr. Biczó picked us for looks as much as for brains? Four times daily—before and after Latin and English—we formed a procession carrying Dr. Biczó's reference books, like bearers in Egyptian hieroglyphs.

During the next four years, while Hitler occupied most of Europe, I spent my recesses in Dr. Biczó's inner sanctum intently discussing art and poetry. Off limits, twentieth-century politics.

We never even mentioned the most vital events affecting Hungary. In April 1941 the prime minister, Pál Teleki, committed suicide rather than join Germany's attack on friendly Yugoslavia, and on June 26 of the same year, Hungary declared war on the Soviet Union as well. Of course, the whole country was shaken by such events, but our school life was hardly affected. In self-defense, we adolescents tried to ignore the growing antisemitism that gripped the gentile populace, most of whom prefered Hitler to Stalin and Nazism to Communism. As for us Jews, we hoped for true democracy, unwilling to admit to ourselves that our goal was nearly hopeless.

• • •

In the political climate of 1940, I was amazed that Dr. Biczó assigned me a major role for the March Fifteenth Festival: I would portray Ilona Zrinyi, the great seventeenth-century heroine. "Do you want to risk it, Jutka?" mother fretted. "Remember what happened two years ago."

"I promised I would, even before Dr. Biczó approached the principal about it. Otherwise, we'd be giving in to the Nazis."

"Of course!" said mother, her eyes kindled. "I'll coach you, and we'll devise a fabulous costume. We'll show them!"

A classmate, Sári Móritz, lent me her mother's heirloom gown for the occasion. My pigtailed, uniformed self was suddenly transformed into a young noblewoman in an ankle-length gown of sea green silk. Next, mother studied Ilona Zrinyi's well-known portrait in my textbook. She fashioned me a similar mantle from my grandmother Klein's gold-appliquéd green velvet tablecloth and braided my long hair with imitation pearls. Perhaps the likeness was intimidating. No one hooted during the performance.

The event ended my childhood. After this public appearance, the boys acted differently. Anti sent me a bouquet of rare mimosa, and I buried my face in the golden puffs. But the very next day a dashing senior from the boys' gimnazium started to trail me on the street. "I prefer him to Anti," I confided to mother as I watched my admirer pace Kontrássy Street in front of our home.

Mother peeked out the window. "He's handsome, Jutka," she allowed, "but remember, he is not Jewish."

"I can't help it if he follows me around," I protested, knowing full well that Jews and gentiles did not mix socially. But the next day I continued to encourage him with wordless smiles.

Eventually, I made inquiries about him, which was easy, since by coincidence most of Dr. Biczó's harem belonged to the prestigious gentry, and so did he. My friend Márta Magay, who was admired for her fairy-tale looks as much as her scholarship, broke the sad news. "He's a senior all right, Jutka," she said, gently patting my arm, "but it's his second time around. He flunked out last year."

I stopped flirting.

• • •

Next year, in 1940, the Jewish holidays were late. Yom Kippur was on October 12. As usual, my uncle Dezső came home from Budapest, and talking animatedly, the Vágó tribe walked along Berzsenyi street to the synagogue together.

Father was an officer at labor service again, and as usual grandpa Vágó stayed at home, making some feeble excuse. Grandfather Klein had been the only pious member of our family, and soon after his death I lost the fervent faith I had. We Jews of Kaposvár, like the Jewry

Portraying the Hungarian heroine, Ilona Zrinyi (1940). The photo was taken outside my grandmother Klein's apartment.

of western and central Hungary, were hardly a devout group, celebrating the high holidays only, and we used to be scolded by our rabbi for being "Yom Kippur Jews"—just as we are in Auburn, Maine, today.

At the main entrance to our neologue[2] synagogue, mother, grandmother Vágó, Magda and I embraced my uncles, then entered the women's more modest door and climbed the winding stairs to the balcony.

My eyes were soon drawn downstairs to the men. They did not all wear the traditional prayer shawls, but they all wore hats: white yarmulkas for the ancients, black bowler hats for the elderly, grey felt for young adults, school caps for adolescents. Of course, I looked for the school caps of the boys' gimnazium and blushed when the tallest tilted toward me. Anti had positioned himself on the opposite side to exchange glances over our prayer books. I smiled, then shook my head: no flirting on the Day of Atonement.

The women's balcony embraced the men's congregation on three sides. Here, too, I could distinguish the hats: matrons in solemn black, young women in bright felt with stylish veils, girls in berets. I wore a white beret pulled to the side Parisian fashion.

Once more my gaze was drawn downstairs, this time to the second row, right. Would father's and grandfather Klein's former seats be taken? They were not. My eyes on their empty bench, I was transported to a past Yom Kippur.

• • •

I am seven or eight, still young enough to pray with the men. Mother has dressed me in a white sailor dress to go to synagogue with father and grandfather Klein, who wears a prayer shawl over his dark suit and a festive black bowler hat. Father lifts me on the bench and shows me the temple all in white: the arc with its gold embroidered lions, the Bible scrolls in their festive garments, the cantor and Rabbi Hercog in their solemn robes. The stained-glass windows lend an unearthly light. Father is cheerful, but O'Papa and I are under the funereal spell. "*Oshamnu,*" we sob in God's own tongue, "we have sinned." I lean against O'Papa's black-suited arm—I am less shy when I stand on the bench—and I strike my chest with my right fist at each confession, boldly like the men: "We have sinned, we have acted falsely, we have been rebellious . . ."

I picture God as a white-haired ancient. He resembles grandfather

2. The small orthodox congregation of Kaposvár met in a hall next door to our large neologue synagogue.

Vágó, but even taller and thinner, leaning on a dark cloud, just above our temple. Before him are two massive books, one in white, the other in black—the Book of Life and the Book of Death. A winged messenger reads off a long sheet of paper. "Judit Magyar has sinned," he frowns, using my formal name. "She has preferred her German to Hebrew. She has been vain. She has been disobedient. She hasn't given her pennies to beggars." I squeeze O'papa's warm hand and chant with him in Hebrew: "Selach lonu—pardon us." His strong voice carries my plea to God. Hurriedly, I add a silent vow: "Dear God, I'll give all my pennies to a beggar child tomorrow." Charity, I had learned in religious class, averts the evil decree. The Almighty reaches for his gold pen and inscribes me in the Book of Life.

•　•　•

My musings about the past were suddenly interrupted. The sonorous chants gave way to expectant silence. Rabbi Hercog mounted the white-clad pulpit and opened his black book of sermons.

"Halt!" a khakhi-clad sergeant burst into the synagogue. "With your permission, Hercog, or without it: official business." Rabbi Hercog leaned against the pulpit, his shoulders visibly shaking. The sergeant pulled out a long sheet of paper. "The following Jews must report to labor service within two hours."

My eyes sought my Vágó uncles. They stood side by side, tall, lean, and wide-shouldered in their dark suits and grey felt hats. Their starched shirts gleamed against their sun-tanned faces.

"Grandmama," I whispered, "is Dezső still registered in the county of Somogy?" Dezső was my favorite; he brought me math puzzles and brain teasers from Budapest.

Grandmother nodded, unable to speak.

The sergeant read from an alphabetical list. My eyes were on my uncles, all in their twenties or thirties. Will they be called? Imre, the youngest, with his romantic eyes. He had fractured an elbow in childhood. Would he be exempt? György, the baker, the only Vágó who hadn't attended the gimnazium. How could grandfather Vágó manage the bakery without him? Andor, the passionate. Could he control his temper? Surely, Andor wasn't cut out for labor camp, much less Dezső, the eldest.

"God help Dezső if he's called to labor service," father had told us before he left. "The man's a genius; the privates will sense that."

"Dear God," I begged, "don't let Dezső be abused by villains."

Their names fell like verdicts: "Vágó Andor; Vágó Dezső; Vágó György; Vágó Imre."

"God forgive me," I prayed in a flash, "I hadn't meant to plead only for Dezső."

When all their names had been read, my uncles left the synagogue together. "God protect them," murmured grandmother Vágó as we hurried down the winding staircase to join them.

During the next four years, our men were periodically called up or dismissed from labor service. I remember their departures mostly. Our sleepy railroad station turned into an army depot, crowded with uniformed Jews with their canary yellow arm bands. Gloved officers strutted about. Ruddy sergeants barked orders, rushing rucksacked Jews into crowded wagons.

Summer or winter, grandmother Vágó shivered, hovering over departing sons. "Don't forget to mend your socks, Dezső," she would beg her eldest, who was most absentminded. "Use those stamped envelopes, György," she would remind the son who was least literary.

We women gathered along the railroad platform to wave our handkerchiefs at a familiar face until it shrank to a dot, then disappeared beyond the bend.

• • •

As Hitler consumed more and more of Europe, the Hungarian government negotiated and renegotiated pacts with Germany. Parliament eventually agreed to several anti-Jewish laws; in exchange, there would be no yellow stars, no ghettos, no deportations.

On August 19, 1941, Parliament voted to deprive all Jews of military rank and my father became a common laborer in an army service unit. He sent home his World War I officer's uniform, and mother unpacked it in tears.

I sent my father a long letter, ending it with a personal plea: "Please, let me get rid of my braids, Papa," I begged. "I'm starting seventh form next month."

Father gave his permission, but ended his letter: "I won't be able to imagine you with short hair."

I had my hair cut, just the same, and sent him a snapshot. His reply was prompt: "My young friend loves it. By the way, we're partners digging ditches." I did not tell father that I had acquired a serious boy friend, a close neighbor of ours, Péter Hanák.

Peti was blond and twenty, a brilliant Jewish student refused from the university by the *numerus clausus,* who had acquired a demanding trade, lathe operator. His Jewish friends, many of them less daring and vigorous than he, used to quote the Hungarian expression about him: "Peti could survive on a sheet of ice." Of course, none of us took this

No more braids (1941). With Ilona and Évi Pogány and their aunt Vilma Solt.

Our class picture (June 1943). 1. Judit Magyar; 2. Évi Kárpáti; 3. Böde Winternitz; 4. Ági Salgó.

literally, but a few years later he was to prove it by surviving a lone march through the frozen Russian steppes. Peti was a cheerful, practical fellow who in his spare time wrote poetry, including love poems. I thought them brilliant, and I still do.

Peti and I had great plans. After the war—and following my graduation from the gimnazium—we would get married, and head for Paris to attend the Sorbonne. We lived on hope, not on fear.

Of course, I couldn't totally ignore the Nazis, much as I shunned the *Somogy Journal.* Hitler bellowed threats on radio and newsreel, vowing to create a "Jew-free" Europe. Few besides father took him literally. Two or three young Jews left Kaposvár before 1941, planning to cross the Yugoslav border illegally.

The war caused hardships for both Jews and gentiles. Imported items, like coffee, were available only on the black market, at unaffordable prices. Basic foodstuffs were rationed. Work and sleep were often interrupted by the screech of sirens. Day or night, we spent tense hours in cellars turned into bomb shelters.

Rumors abounded. We heard of Jews from all over Europe being dragged to Dachau, a German concentration camp. "Rubbish," declared Dr. Ármuth, our family physician, a decorated hero of World War I and therefore exempt from the Jewish laws. "How could that many Jews fit into a single camp?" he argued, convincingly. "They imprison political prisoners only."

In the summer of 1943, one scary rumor followed another; we tried to ignore them. Soon after our graduation ceremonies from the gimnazium, I heard of Italian Jews being shipped through our own Kaposvár railroad station. "The things people dream up," sighed Dr. Ármuth's pretty wife, Manyi, who dropped by for a visit.

"What if it's true?" I interjected. "I've heard that babies were begging for water through the cracks."

"Don't believe everything you hear, Jutka," mother tried to calm me with a phrase I'd been hearing much too often lately.

"But Jewish girls are being dragged to the Russian front by cattle cars," I retorted. "Imre and Andor have seen *them.*"

"That's different," mother shuddered. "It's horrid, but different. Why should they take little children? It doesn't make sense."

"That's just what my husband said," smiled Mrs. Ármuth.

This time I tended to agree with them, but the image of cattle cars stuffed with thirsty people lingered until next July, when I shared one of them.

4
OUR GENERAL
Kaposvár, Hungary • Spring 1944

I WAS eighteen when Hitler occupied Hungary.

The regent Horthy, who had been sustaining a degree of internal independence by cooperating with Hitler's armies, had recently embarked on secret negotiations with the Allied forces. As Hitler discovered this, he ordered the occupation of Hungary.

Early on that fateful morning of March 19, 1944, I woke to thunder crashing over our roof. Thunder in spring? Impossible! Hands over my ears, I leaped to the window. The sky over Kaposvár was armored in steel. "The Americans!" I rejoiced, running to my parents' room. "They've come!"

Father was away in the army's labor service; mother stood alone by the window, frail in her nightgown. She pointed at the planes. I saw Hitler's swastikas, and felt weak in the knees. German bombers hung wing to wing, their bellies scraping the chimneys. No sirens. No anti-aircraft. The Germans were allies. By noon, Hitler had Hungary under his feet. Governor Horthy seemed powerless, parliamentary procedures were abandoned, and a daily succession of "Jewish ordinances" filled the *Somogy Journal*.

Three weeks later, mother and I were having breakfast by the cold stove. "Have something to eat, Mama," I passed the bread basket.

"You take it, Jutka," she murmured. "I'm not hungry this morning." Mother was never hungry when father was away, but rationing had increased my appetite. I devoured the bread in quick gulps.

"Shall I make a fire?" I offered.

"Save the firewood, Jutka," mother cautioned. "Who knows? We might still be around this winter. Have you seen this, Jutka?" Mother pushed the *Somogy Journal* across the table. The headline screamed in bold black letters: "FIRST DAY OF THE DAVID STAR."

"Why call it David Star?" I mumbled. Our Jewish leaders had forewarned us of the necessity to wear a yellow star, a throwback to the Middle Ages. Scowling, I read the rest:

> Today, April 6TH, 1944, a new epoch began. Starting this morning, all Jews over six years of age—and Christians designated as Jews by the Jewish laws—must wear the yellow star in times of peace as well as war. The star must be prominently displayed on the left breast, 9cm. in diameter. of canary yellow velvet, wool or cotton. It is to be worn in all public places, streets, shops and bomb shelters.

"Bomb shelters!" I exclaimed. "They never miss a thing."

I got up to gather our dishes, but mother held me back. "Listen, Jutka, I couldn't sleep last night, I was so worried. The town is full of German soldiers: I'm sure Papa wouldn't let you out with that yellow star."

"Oh, Papa," I shrugged. "He'd lock me up in the nunnery if he could!"

"That may not be such a bad idea," mother countered.

"C'mon, Mama!" I protested. "You've never panicked before. I must go to work." I was apprenticed to a Mr. Szilárd, the foremost dental technician in town, and I took my apprenticeship seriously. By next September, I hoped to support myself as a part-time dental technician in Paris, while attending the Sorbonne.

"I'll wear my old winter coat," I offered, and after some more debate, mother sewed my yellow star on it.

"Lucky it's a cold day," she murmured, handing me a black knitted cap. "Pull it over your eyebrows, Jutka." She hugged me as for a long journey.

My workplace was a ten-minute walk from home. The once-friendly houses stared at me with shuttered eyes. There won't even be a witness—I shuddered as I dashed uphill on Kontrássy Street. Children streaming toward the convent school on Zárda Ucca—Nunnery Street—pointed their fingers at my yellow star. A matronly nun in an ankle-length black habit stood by the gate, her large, white headdress flapping in the breeze. Spotting my star, she crossed herself, murmuring a prayer.

German soldiers paid no attention to me, and I felt safer, until a ragged boy spit into my face on Kossuth Square: "Stinking Jew girl!"

Never mind the urchin—I told myself, wiping my face as I turned up onto Fő Ucca.

"No trouble on the streets, Jutka?" Mr. Szilard asked me as I entered. "I hardly expected to see you this morning."

On my way home that afternoon, I found Fő Ucca in full swing. The promenade! How could I have forgotten it? Young people were strutting and flirting in their spring coats and military dress uniforms as if nothing else mattered. Of course, I was no longer a part of this pageant, but I felt self-conscious with my outgrown winter coat and my yellow star. A couple of former classmates crossed the street to avoid meeting me, but Márta Magay sailed toward me with arms extended: "Jutka!"

"Márti," I whispered, turning away, "you'll be arrested!"

Márta's arms fell as if sawed off at the shoulders.

•   •   •

I met mother by the gate, just coming home from work; she held father's accountant's position at Hónig & Weinberger at a fraction of his former pay—the maximum allowed under the Third Jewish Law.

"Thank God, Jutka!" she embraced me. "I'm on my way to see mama and papa before it's dark. D'you want to come? I suppose it's safe enough."

The Vágó establishment was only a few blocks away, on Berzsenyi Street. The tantalizing aroma of fresh bread met us at the door, but grandfather's shop stood depleted. Even *komisz kenyér*—mean bread, the army ration bread, was sold out.

My grandparents were having their afternoon coffee at the ends of the long family table. Grandfather displayed his yellow star on his crumpled jacket, grandmother wore hers on her grey flannel dress. In case of customers, I supposed. Despite grandmother's fancy Hungarian cooking, they had been bony ever since I could remember them. They seemed unusually gaunt today. I embraced them in turn: grandmother's cheeks were clammy, grandfather's mustache tickled. "Sit down, sit down," grandfather gestured. "Pour them some coffee, Józsa."

Mother and I were sipping the ersatz coffee when my aunt Magda entered in a huge black coat, a grey knitted shawl hiding her face. The yellow star glared, prominent.

"We're sold out!" yelled grandfather.

"Papa," laughed Magda, taking off her coat. "It's me! In my mother-in-law's trappings. Poor dear, she's trying to protect me from the Germans."

"You girls shouldn't have come," murmured grandmother. Magda bent lithely for an embrace. I glanced at her, admiringly: how romantic she looks in a simple brown dress, like a Spanish Madonna in a Murillo painting. People said that I resembled my young aunt Magda, but I was

My aunt Magda (1937). ". . . more like a sister than an aunt."

In the Kaposvár ghetto (June 1944). My maternal grandparents, Józsa and Lajos Vágó, with my mother, shortly before grandfather's death and our deportation.

more down to earth, she more mysterious. Her brown eyes flashed as she pulled out a letter.

"From Feri?" I asked, my face heating. I still thought of them as honeymooners; they were married for only a few months before the young husband, Ferenc Rosenberger, left for labor camp three years ago.

"Look at you blushing," Magda teased. She was only twenty-seven, more like a sister than an aunt.

"Any news from the men?" Magda asked, pulling up a cane-backed chair.

Grandmother's lips quivered: "Nothing from the boys. Nothing."

"Józsa, listen," boomed grandfather, "tell them about our house guests."

Grandmother's pale lips eased into a smile. "A couple of young men got billeted with us this morning."

"Men!" cried mother. "Do you mean German soldiers?"

Grandmother blinked, massaging her fingers. "Just a couple of starved boys, really. Their mothers must be worried."[1]

"Grandmama!" I crimsoned. "You aren't going to feed them?"

"Don't worry," waved grandfather. "They'll probably bring their rations."

"That's not the point, Papa," mother objected.

Grandmother's puffed eyes flooded with tears. "I only pray some kind woman would feed my own boys."

Suddenly, heavy steps approached from the courtyard. "Good-bye, everyone!" I cried, grabbing my coat. Too late! The door swung open. A robust German sergeant pushed his huge boot across the threshold, dripping mud on grandmother's oiled floor.

Grandfather stared at the dirty boot, at the disgusting puddle. "Wipe your feet!" he yelled in pidgin German. "Where are your manners?"

"Shut up, Jew-filth!" the sergeant's hand flew to his pistol.

"Can't you see?" grandfather said calmly. "My wife's too weak to scrub the floors. Haven't you a mother back home?"

The gun slipped back into its holster, and grumbling, the sergeant headed toward the corridor.

Two skinny privates now followed him in across the threshold, busily wiping their boots on grandmother's cocoa mat. In their over-

---

1. Despite the ban on fraternization between "Aryans" and Jews, scores of German soldiers were billeted in Jewish homes.

sized uniforms they looked like costumed children. Fifteen or sixteen years old, I thought. Hitler can't last much longer.

"Küss die Hand, Gnädige Frau," they bowed.

"Grüss Gott," grandmother nodded.

"When is supper, please?" asked the taller boy.

"I'll fix it soon," grandmother smiled, her face lighting. "You boys look starved. I'll bring you some rolls and coffee in a minute." With light steps belying her rheumatism, grandmother disappeared into her kitchen. I listened, closing my eyes, to the familiar sounds of male boots echoing along the corridor.

"Papa, you should be more careful," mother said after she shut the door. "That murderer might have killed you on the spot."

"Of course not," grandfather waved it off. "I'm still in charge of this household."

"You don't understand, Papa," Magda protested. "We have no recourse against them."

Grandfather pulled his gaunt frame to its full six feet. Under his aquiline nose, a white hussar mustache dared the world and all the Germans in it. "What's the point of being scared?" he slapped his strong baker's hand on his yellow star. "Look at me, women. See this gold star? I've been promoted to a general!"

I burst out laughing, but Magda shook her head: "It's no joking matter, Papa."

Grandfather folded his creaky joints back to the table, and faced each of us in turn. "Listen to me, Rózsi, Magda, Jutka. Listen! Don't be afraid to speak to any man. Soldiers may be beasts on the battlefield, but they all had a mother, just like you and me."

"You're right, Papa." mother said, squeezing his thick-veined hand. "I'll remember that."

"I know just what you mean," Magda nodded.

I, too, nodded my head, but I wished I knew how to implement it. I wanted to ask, but I was too embarrassed: could I convince a German soldier not to rape me? Through the closed door I heard the clicking of crockery: grandmother was serving coffee.

The German occupation soon transformed me from a law-abiding, cautious schoolgirl into a devil-may-care subversive. If the authorities called Jews to a daily duel, I met it. Each day, they wanted specifics: lard, sugar, flour, rice, beans. Hiding became an obsession. Jewish ration cards had been severely cut, and starvation was a real threat. The Vágó establishment had plenty of hiding places, from cellars to attics, all familiar to me from childhood games of hide-and-go-seek. Soon I had the whole establishment for my clandestine activities. The bakery was closed, all machinery having been confiscated, and grandmother Vágó's German soldiers had departed for the Russian front—having surprised her with a "certificate for good hospitality."

When the order came to submit our gold and silver, we collected all our family valuables in the middle of the big oak table, and divided them into three small heaps: one for the Germans, one for the transport, one to bury under the rose bush. I picked my small signet ring for the rose bush.

"My God!" mother exclaimed. "I almost forgot Jani's signet ring; he gave it to me for safekeeping. Quick! Get it, Jutka." I ran for the familiar ring, inherited from father to son.

Reverently, I buried the family mementos in their tin coffin, under the rose bush. When I returned from the courtyard, grandmother Vágó had her gold ring and her locket watch in her palm. "I *must* give them my wedding ring," she grieved. "And I'll give them the chain. But not the watch; it was my engagement present, and has kept perfect time these forty-five years."

"No wonder," grumbled grandfather Vágó. "I paid good money for it. Hide it in the stove, Józsa. There are still some ashes in it." And so we hid grandmother's locket under the ashes, together with some rings.

My toughest challenge came on May 1. "Jews must submit their radios, typewriters, and bicycles for the war effort," the Nazis ordered.

"Not my bike," I vowed. "Not my typewriter." Since our radio had been registered, I stood in line a whole day to get the receipt for it—as I had done with the silver and the gold. Next morning, I pedaled to an isolated little house, white against the dark Cser forest. A former classmate lived there. I came to the point at once: "You haven't got a bike, have you?" She shook her head. "D'you want to ride mine? I'll take it back after the war is over."

She glanced at my yellow star: "I hope you make it, Jutka."

"If I don't, it's yours," I said, suddenly feeling threatened.

"It's a deal," she grabbed the handlebars.

"Watch out," I warned her, quoting the papers: "No mercy to Christians who hide Jew property."

"I'm aware of it," she shrugged it off. "Please run along, Jutka, before anyone sees us."

My typewriter presented a more serious problem; middle-class girls did not own them. Mine was an exception, a pooled graduation present from my four Vágó uncles in lieu of books, clothes, or jewels. I decided to take it to Ági Toronyi: she was both well-to-do and daring. Despite the curfew and mother's protests, I sneaked it off to Agi Toronyi's house after dark.

Ági's father answered the bell. "Who's there?"

"It's me, Jutka Magyar."

"What are you doing here?"

"Please, Dr. Toronyi," I begged, "I need your help." Did his obstetrician's eyes mistake the protrusion under my coat? He let me in. Pulling out my machine, I asked for Ági.

She ran down in her pajamas. "Jutka!"

"Shh," Dr. Toronyi cautioned. "The maids!" Father and daughter held a hushed debate in the hall, while I hugged my typewriter like a pet.

"Enough of this!" Dr. Toronyi hissed, as a door banged upstairs. "Put it on your desk, Ági. Pray God, we never regret it." Quickly, he checked the street and pushed me out. "Run along!"

"Thanks!" I called to the slamming door. Did I feel guilty for endangering my friend? Not the least bit. I had tricked the Germans and was proud of it. "Lucky," I winked at the blinking stars. "Lucky, lucky!" The curfew was still in effect, but I skipped down Eszterházy Street, humming to myself. I shall never be caught. I felt sure of it.

• • •

By May 1944, love was nurtured only by correspondence. I thought myself lucky, for ever since my boyfriend, Peti Hanák, had left town for labor service, he had kept me enchanted with excellent letters. But unfortunately—or fortunately as it turned out later—I had hardly seen him since age seventeen, and my love for him remained adolescent.

On May 25 a ghetto was established in my hometown, just as if time had reversed to the Middle Ages. "The barbed wired gates will shut in the Jews" was the way the *Somogy Journal* put it. Mother, Magda, and I moved into my grandparents' home at number 45 Berzsenyi Street, which, luckily for us, became the ghetto's main street. Four families shared the house, not all of them related.

Soon, there were rumors of Jewish women being transported to the Russian front as forced prostitutes to German soldiers. It was said that married women would be exempt, which pressured us girls to wed. The weddings were pro forma, hastily performed at City Hall. Only Évi Kárpáti's was officiated by Rabbi Hercog. Évi married her love, Laci Faludi, who happened to be home on a furlough. Most people thought them fortunate, but I mourned for my friend. "Too many eyes in the ghetto," Évi complained, "we can't escape them."

Ilona Pogány faced a different threat. She was being pressured to enter a pro forma marriage with a cousin. "Surely, Jancsi won't take advantage," I urged her.

"Of course not," Ilona gently protested, "but I'll marry Pali and nobody else." Pali had been missing from the Russian front for more than a year, probably dead, but Ilona expected him home any day.

As for me, I would have preferred a pro forma wedding with an uncle, rather than a hasty honeymoon with my boyfriend. Love by correspondence seemed poor preparation for sex, and a honeymoon in the ghetto was totally repulsive. As it turned out, neither my uncles nor Peti got a furlough before all of our ghetto's inhabitants were transported to Auschwitz.

• • •

Soon after our move to my grandparents' house, we had our last gentile visitor, the wiry Ulrich, a baker's helper from another part of town, who once worked for grandfather as an apprentice. "Is the old man at home?" he asked me crisply, striding through the cluttered shop.

"Grandfather is out in the courtyard," I said, and trailed him there. Grandfather was reading his newspaper under his favorite tree, its wide branches laden with apricots, round and small, green with promise.

"*Jó napot*—Good day," Ulrich mumbled, without tipping his hat.

"*Jó napot*," gasped grandfather, taken by surprise. "How come you visit a Jew?"

"I have permission," Ulrich announced, his foxy chin held high. "I came to measure the premises. The house and the bakery'll soon be mine. Let's start with the rooms."

"Józsa!" yelled grandfather. Grandmother's worn face soon appeared at the kitchen window. "Ulrich wants to say something to you."

"What is it?" she wanted to know.

"Tell her," grandfather beckoned to the baker. "You used to eat her cooking. Remember?" Grandmother always fed the help with the same excellent food she cooked for her family, which was unusual.

"*Jó napot*, Mrs. Vágó," bowed an abashed Ulrich, politely enough. "D'you mind if I look at your rooms?"

"*My* rooms?" complained grandmother. "A different family in every one. Some haven't even made their beds yet. Can you believe it?"

"Never mind, Mrs. Vágó," Ulrich soothed. "Let's not bother." Grandmother's head disappeared into the kitchen. Ulrich turned back to grandfather: "Will you show me the bakery, old man?"

"The bakery?" grandfather grunted. "I padlocked it. Damn Nazis! They took all my machinery."

"I know," said Ulrich, suppressing a grin. "Don't you curse them."

"Haha!" thundered grandfather, eyeing him over his spectacles. "I get it: you joined the Nazis, yourself! Did they give you my machinery too?"

"How else could I get a bakery of my own?" retorted Ulrich. "Anyways, you should have retired by now. Eighty, aren't you?"

"Eighty-three," bragged grandfather, getting up from his bentwood chair. "And not a sick day in my life. You try and match that."

"Why not?" said Ulrich. "I'm halfway there." He measured the rambling buildings, peeked in at the windows, counted the fruit trees, and paced out the large vegetable garden with his spindly legs. "It's a fine place," he grinned, returning.

"You want it free," grandfather eyed him, "but I built it from scratch fifty years ago. And by God, I'm still the master here."

"Not for long," said Ulrich. "A train is on its way, old man. You people will be on a transport before these apricots ripen."

Grandfather touched a baby apricot with a trembling finger. "I won't leave this house alive," he murmured. "Never."

"Sorry, Uncle Vágó," Ulrich shrugged his shoulders. "It's out of my hands. You Jews will soon leave and you won't come back, either. No use hiding your valuables."

"I'll never leave this house alive," grandfather repeated. "Want to bet?"

"It's a bet," Ulrich said.

Ulrich's predictions had been foreshadowed by our Jewish Council—the governing body formed at the order of the Germans as was their custom. The council advised us to pack our rucksacks before moving to the ghetto "in case there is a transport." Grandfather had refused to have anything to do with a backpack. "I am too old to be a Boy Scout," he grumbled.

A week or so later, on June 4th, I was on my way to the ghetto's only grocery with a wicker basket on my arm, since we couldn't go beyond the barbed wire fence. Halfway to the store, I spotted a former classmate, Ági Salgó. She was dressed ghetto style, with an apron and a kerchief, which was our way to save on washing and shampooing. I had never seen Ági with an apron, much less with a kerchief—her father, Dr. Sándor Salgó, a retired professor from the Kaposvár Business Academe, used to be strict about "ladylike" appearance. Ági dared not contradict her father, because bedridden Dr. Salgó was easily thrown into depression.

Ági bubbled today, her usually plain face embellished by the flush of excitement. "Jutka! Jutka! Such great news!"

"What happened?"

"Haven't you seen the papers?"

"Hitler surrendered?"

"Almost," she beamed. "The Americans landed in Normandy!"

"Thank God!" I embraced her. "The war is almost over!"

We discussed the likelihood of school by September—Ági at the University of Budapest, I at the Sorbonne—until I remembered my family: "I must run home to tell them! The Americans landed in Europe! Imagine that!"

Starting that day, it seemed to us that American bombers flashed across the Kaposvár skies more and more often, winging in silver streaks toward Austria. Occasional bombing had occurred in Hungary by then, but so far Kaposvár had escaped it. We did not have enough bomb shelters for all the ghetto's inhabitants, but I wasn't worried. At the first blast of the sirens I would run out to the courtyard, wildly waving my arms: "Hurry, Americans! Hurry!"

Early in June, on an especially hot afternoon, grandfather Vágó collapsed in the courtyard. I ran for Dr. Lővy, a fine physician and mother's childhood sweetheart. After a thorough examination, Dr. Lővy told us that grandfather had fallen into a coma.

"I can't believe it!" grandmother Vágó cried out, kneading her bony fingers. "He had never been sick. Why now? At the worst possible moment!"

"Perhaps it's for the best, Aunt Vágó," sighed Dr. Lővy. "Let's pray he'll die in his own bed."

Soon, grandfather's bed reeked of refuse and ruin, despite the constant change of linen. In the stale room, around the deathbed, we gathered nightly to pack and repack our rucksacks.

Grandmother used Imre's small Boy Scout pack but filled it only partway. Magda noticed it first. "Bring me your winter coat, Mama," she suggested. "I'll stick it into my own pack."

"I won't need it," grandmother shook her head.

"Grandmama," I protested, "let Magda take it for you. I'll carry the rest: your hat, gloves, overshoes. A warm dress and a sweater. The war may last into winter."

"I know," grandmother sighed. "But I won't."

As for me, I feared rape more than death and I decided to take some poison with me. Mother coaxed it out of Mr. Mittelman, a kind pharmacist and member of the Jewish Council. Sadly, she divided it into five small bags, one for each of us. Next, mother considered the gold teeth she had bought from a dentist's widow as a hedge against inflation. "Here, Jutka, take a couple of bridges to Ica and Nana Klein," she suggested. Grandmother Klein shared a tiny room with aunt Ica next door; I stuffed the forbidden gold into my apron pocket and ran over with it.

"No, thanks, Jutka," Nana pursed her lips, pushing the gold back into my pocket. "Ica and I won't barter."

My aunt had set up a miniature kitchen in a corner, where she was stirring some farina on an electric plate. Grandmother's knick-knacks and Herend bowls were everywhere in the cluttered little room, but grandfather's silver cigar trays were missing. They had been given to the Germans.

Grandmother pulled out her heavy sealskin coat from her rucksack. "I've sewn a bit of jewelry into the shoulder pads," she told me conspiringly. "A neighbor suggested it."

"Nana," I protested, lifting the heavy fur. "It weighs a ton. You aren't going to lug this on a transport? Grandmother Vágó will travel light."

"I'm not your grandmother Vágó," Nana flustered. "I'll take it, if I take nothing else. Papa gave it to me on our twenty-fifth anniversary. Thank God, he didn't live to see this," she sighed as she looked around the cluttered room in despair. "Once more the fugitive."

"Grandpapa is well out of it," I embraced her tiny form. "I must go now, Nana. The garden is waiting. D'you want some strawberries for supper? I'll bring you a basketful with the peas."

"Thanks, Jutka. I don't know what we'd do without the Vágós' garden. But wait a minute. I must talk to you about your inheritance."

"My inheritance, Nana?" I burst out laughing. "At a time like this?"

"Stay, Jutka," aunt Ica urged me. "The jewelry has been much on Mama's mind lately. The transport, you know. Preparing . . ."

"Listen, Jutka," grandmother turned solemn, "I'm leaving the jewelry to Ica, but I want your mother to have my garnet brooch, and I want *you* to have the pearl ring Papa bought me the day you were born. First grandchild, you know . . . What a scrawny thing. Dear, dear, who would have thought you'd outgrow us all? And I want you to have . . ."

"Nana," I interrupted, admiring my aunt Ica for her patience, "I must help grandmama Vágó with the peas. But the idea of shoulder pads is great. It's really great, Nana!"

That night, we carefully ripped our coats apart and sewed the gold bridges into the bulky pads, but next morning, when we discovered that the idea had spread the length of the ghetto, we took apart the coats again and decided to hide the gold in tooth paste. After midnight, Magda fetched grandfather Vágó's hammer and broke the bridges into individual teeth. Mother skillfully stuffed them into four tubes with the help of a match stick.

Magda's pounding woke grandfather, and he asked feebly for water. He never spoke again, except the day the movers came to cart the furniture away.

According to the newspapers, the confiscated goods would be shipped to help out victims of recent bombardments, but as I found out later, most of it was grabbed by Nazi opportunists before it left Kaposvár.

The Jewish Council had prepared us for this intrusion, but grandmother Vágó panicked the moment the men attacked her bed. "No!" she shrieked.

Grandfather raised a corpselike head. "What's this?" he mumbled, waking from the coma. His sunken eyes met grandmother's bed swinging in midair, its corner scraping the ceiling. Slowly, painstakingly, he murmured: "We first slept in it . . . forty-four years ago . . . today."

"My God," choked grandmother. "Papa knows the date!"

"The tenth of June," Magda whispered. "Your anniversary."

As the bed reached the door, grandmother sadly informed the men: "My six children and my granddaughter were born in that bed."

The movers dropped the bed with a crash and made the sign of the cross. "It's not our fault," said the younger, a redhead. "We've been hired to do a job."

They tiptoed back to grandfather, who had fallen into a coma again. "We'll leave him his bed," whispered the older man. They lugged out its twin, the bureaus and night tables we emptied hurriedly, and came back for the chairs. "You're allowed to keep one chair per person," said the bald one. "Which ones d'you want?"

Grandmother was sitting at grandfather's side, her face in her palms. "Leave us four dining chairs," she murmured.

"What about the old man?" offered the redhead.

Grandmother raised her eyes to the half-empty room, her gaze fleeing to the window. Outside, the courtyard gleamed in a green light. "Leave me his bentwood under the apricot tree," she sighed.

Late that evening we rummaged in our rucksacks in the bare room. From time to time grandfather let out a gurgle, the only sound. The air reeked of urine again. "I'll take a breath of fresh air," I said and escaped to the moonlit courtyard. Crouching on the wooden steps, I rehearsed the contents of my pack. A tin box held some carefully chosen papers and photographs—including my gimnazium diploma. What if I had to abandon it on a forced march?

Quickly, I returned to the room. "Someone find me a candle," I told my surprised family. "I'm going to reopen the cellar cave and stuff in my papers and snapshots. Anything else you want to hide?"

"What about the jewelry in the stove?" mother remembered. She scraped the tin cookie box from the ashes, and handed it to me: "Take it, Jutka."

A few minutes later, I climbed down a rickety ladder to the root cellar. "I'll stand guard," Magda offered, handing me a candle. Painstakingly, I reopened the brick wall that supported the kitchen wall. The urn of goose fat stood in the cave I had dug for it a week or two before. I placed my two tin boxes on top of it, and replaced the bricks, carefully pushing sand into all the cracks. Next, I cleaned up the candle drippings. Climbing up the ladder, I felt triumphant, and rightly so. The contents of that cave—including most of the photographs that appear in this book—were all that remained to us after the war.

It was near dawn when Magda and I got back to our room, but mother and grandmother were still at their rucksacks. "Let's stop all this packing," I groaned. "Go to sleep, everyone. I'll watch over grandpapa." The three women curled up on some blankets and I took my turn at grandfather's bedside. He lay motionless, his breath suddenly faint. His fleshless skull shone in the dim light, a delicate sculpting. A saying from Michelangelo came to my mind: declaring the skull of even the lowliest beggar a more elaborate structure than the dome of the Pantheon.

My grandfather was dying; I sat stooped at the edge of his bed, trying to say good-bye to him. But pity escaped me. If only this ordeal would end, I thought desperately. If only grandpapa would die. If only we were deported. Anything but this waiting.

A few days later, American planes roared low over Kaposvár, nearly touching the rooftops. Mother, Magda, and I dashed to the hall and threw ourselves under the table. On our return, we found grandmother weeping by the bed. Grandfather was dead. I tried to pray with my family, but Ulrich's image kept interfering. Silently, I congratulated grandfather Vágó—he had won his wager.

5
HUMANS AND
APRICOTS

Kaposvár, Hungary • June 1944

O N a blazing morning in June 1944, four yellow-starred women
emerged from the Kaposvár ghetto.

My friends envied me this morning's exit. "A pass to leave the
ghetto," they marveled. "Imagine that." Ilona alone mourned for the
dead: "Poor, poor uncle Vágó." But I felt relieved: Grandpapa wouldn't
be threatened by a transport. He won his bet, had his final victory over
the Nazis.

Évi Kárpáti ran to the closing gate to call after me: "Take a good
look around, Jutka. And say hello to Lajos Kossuth for me!" Lajos Kossuth, patriot, liberal, was the father of the Hungarian revolution of
1848. His statue guarded the main square of most towns, including
Kaposvár's.

I let mother and Magda support grandmother Vágó as I trailed
after them—watching, recording, like an uninvolved observer. Kontrássy Street was alive with former neighbors. But no one greeted us,
no one even made a sign of recognition, just as if the yellow star had
made us invisible. Of course, they were rightfully scared and perhaps
embarrassed, but "Cowards," I fumed, borrowing their eyes to view our
procession. They averted their eyes—ants whose hill had not been
crushed, I figured.

I fell behind my family and stopped for a moment. The main
square pained me. To my right, kerchiefed farm wives squatted by
their baskets in the bustling outdoor market—timeless, indifferent. To
my left, immense cannas flaunted their brilliant skirts as if nothing

shameful were happening—yellow and red, yellow and red. Straight ahead, Lajos Kossuth's fatherly statue greeted me with a raised hand. "Patience," it seemed to say, "history changes."

Dr. Biczó's motto came to mind from Latin class: "Tempora mutantur, et nos mutamur in illis.—Times change and we change with them." Had Dr. Biczó changed with the Nazi times? Would he attend papa Vágó's funeral? How about my former classmates? I imagined a crowd waiting for us by the cemetery gates. I mustn't speak, I reminded myself, I'll just nod in their direction. I caught up with my family to ask: "Who'll come, d'you think?"

"Papa's gentile card partners, surely," said mother. "They must have seen the death notice in the *Somogy Journal*. Such a pity we couldn't give papa a decent funeral."

Stepping along Fő Ucca, I glanced around. The Jewish shops mourned with padlocked shutters. "Sunt lacrimae rerum—There are tears for things," I remembered from the *Aeneid,* amazed to be reminded of school again. Climbing the steep hill on upper Fő Ucca, I recalled grandfather Klein's funeral, shuddering at the contrast: the snow-clad streets, the elegant cortège, the line of sleighs, Mayor Kaposvári with his entourage. Today, Mayor Kaposvári refused Rabbi Hercog a pass to attend the funeral.

"If only Imre could come," panted grandmother Vágó, doubled from the steep climb. "If only he could come . . ." Our men were far away—father, Magda's Feri, and three of my Vágó uncles at the Russian front. Only Imre, the youngest, was nearby, recently restationed to an army labor camp near Kaposvár. We had sent him a message with a Jew on furlough.

"Imre will come," I said, suddenly optimistic. "He'll be waiting for us by the gate, you'll see."

But no one waited, except the simple coffin on a horse-drawn cart with a sleepy driver. Silently, he swung open the iron grille doors and he helped us carry the light coffin to its fresh-dug site. Two old women in ample black skirts and chin-tied kerchiefs knelt by the open grave. "A Greek Chorus," I whispered to Magda, "it fits the tragedy." Their wrinkled hands moved rosary beads from finger to finger. Grandmother Vágó stepped ahead to greet Mrs. Hottó, our Catholic washerwoman who had come with her sister, but mother reminded her that we were forbidden to speak to them.

"Shouldn't we say some prayers?" I suggested.

"Not yet! Not yet!" Grandmother Vágó begged. "Imre must say the Kaddish." And turning toward the driver, she told him, once more forgetting the restrictions: "We're waiting for my son. It's the son's duty to say the funeral prayers." The driver pretended not to hear her, but he let us stay.

In the silent cemetery, the kneeling women mumbled the Lord's Prayer: ". . . give us this day our daily bread and forgive us our trespasses as we forgive those who trespass against us . . ." "There are so many to forgive," I thought, "the words fit."

Soon, we spotted Imre running toward us on his long legs. Panting, my uncle told us he had risked his life to come, bribing a guard to leave camp and riding a train in the men's toilet. After the Kaddish, Imre rushed to catch the next train back to his labor camp.

Why didn't he join the partisans? Because none existed. Why didn't he escape to the woods across the borders? Because the Germans were everywhere, surrounding the country as well. There was no place to hide, except the men's toilet.

Before he left, my young uncle took me aside for a moment; by a stranger's tombstone, he grabbed my hand. "Jutka," he said, "don't forget what I told you about the Russian front."

"I've had plenty of nightmares about it."

"It can't be helped," he said, squeezing my hand. "Jewish girls get mass-raped and buried alive; I saw them, digging their own graves. I don't know where you could hide, Jutka. But you must. Risk your life to escape a girls' transport. Promise me that."

I looked into his eyes, shaped like my own. "I promise," I said.

•   •   •

When we returned to the ghetto, a boy was waiting for me in the courtyard. "Judit Magyar!" he called. "Come, quick! It's a gentleman."

"A gentleman," I repeated, surprised. "A Christian?"

He nodded. Who could it be, I wondered, as I followed him to the ghetto fence. Who would risk internment for me? A nervous Dr. Biczó was striding along the free side. "Oh no!" he gasped at my yellow star.

"Dr. Biczó," I said, "you shouldn't have come."

"I brought you something," he muttered, pushing a book over the barbed wire. Quickly, I glanced up Berzsenyi Street. No danger. I grabbed the slim volume and slipped it into my apron pocket.

"It is Plato's *Gorgias,*" he murmured. "Remember?"

"Socrates!" I nodded. "Of course I remember!"

"This time it is yours to keep."

"Thanks," I said, hand on my apron pocket. "I'll take it with me if there's a transport."

"That's why I came," he bit his lower lip. "Mayor Kaposvári told me it may be imminent. Please, give my heartfelt wishes to Magda Vágó and to all my former students." He turned away to wipe his eyes, then grabbed my hand through the fence. "Good-bye, Judit Magyar," he whispered. "I hope . . ." But he choked into silence.

"Good-bye, Dr. Biczó," I said, feeling condemned.

It was dangerous for him to stay by the fence, but he did not turn to go. When I glanced back, Dr. Biczó was there still—a statue of himself, one foot posed before the other. But the image was fragmented by the barbed wire fence.

• • •

A week later, just before sunset, I crouched outdoors on my rucksack, reading the *Gorgias,* when ten ancients wrapped in prayer shawls came to recite the Kaddish—the prayer for the dead. "Thank God, the week of Mazkir is over," I whispered to Magda, sniffing their smell of age and sweat.

"Has papa been buried for a week?" Magda shivered, and suddenly I imagined grandfather's corpse mouldy in its coffin.

The old men bowed and chanted before grandfather Vágó's empty bed; grandmother, mother, Magda, and I squatted on orange crates, the traditional seats of mourning. The Nazis had left our four chairs—occupied by Nana Klein, aunt Ica, and two elderly friends—mother's baby picture above the lonely bed, and our rucksacks in the corner. How soon before we strap them on? Tomorrow, perhaps? Dr. Biczó said the transport might be imminent.

The old men's Kaddish became a loud lament: it had become a funeral prayer for the living as well. I left my wooden crate with a shiver, tiptoed out of the room, and fled to the courtyard.

Grandfather's bentwood chair leaned against his apricot tree, just as he had left it. The tree was filled with apricots, ripened since grandfather fell into a coma. The chair, though gnarled and stiff as grandfather had been, received me kindly as I sank down.

A luminous sky lent its glow to the courtyard. As the last rays of the sun flooded the apricot tree, my eyes leapt to a golden apricot over my shoulder, and back to my shoulder, curving under the apricot. The same rounded design. The same golden fuzz. We were the same stuff, humans and apricots.

The sun slipped away. The curtain was down. My foot nudged a fallen fruit, lying in the grass. It oozed apart. In the dim light I lifted my cotton skirt. My eyes skipped from thighs to fruit, from fruit to thighs. "We'll die and rot," I murmured.

The next morning we got our orders for deportation.

• • •

At 8 A.M. on July 2, 1944, we were given four hours to pack, but our rucksacks were ready. "Let's cook a decent meal," said grandmother Vágó, "the beans and raspberries are perfect." Grandmother and I had tended the garden since the closing of the ghetto, and the first batch of wax beans had ripened just in time for this meal—yellow, tender, and velvety. Mother had planned to cook them "french style" with some vinegar and hoarded sugar, but at the last minute, grandmother Vágó spooned in a small jar of her precious apricot jam. "No use saving it for the boys," she murmured.

Grandmother and I were doing the dishes, when mother entered. "You forgot to sweep the hall this morning," grandmother reminded her.

"Who cares?" mother retorted. "And why do you wipe those plates, Mama? Smash them to the floor, instead!" Grandmother's worn hand trembled in mid-air, her eyes begging for pity. "Sorry, Mama," mother whispered, "I'll sweep the hall right away." And so it was that we left the place neat and clean for Mrs. Ulrich.

Before we donned our rucksacks, grandmother bent to stroke the cat: "What about you, poor thing? Who'll feed you now?" The cat rubbed, mewing, against grandmother's ankle, then leaped on the apricot tree and yowled uncontrollably.

•   •   •

It was a humiliating day. At the synagogue, male officials examined our packs, ruthlessly grabbing anything that took their fancy. Grandmother Vágó presented her "certificate for good hospitality," but to no avail: we lost our soap, our chocolate, our hand-knit sweaters and Nana Klein's sealskin coat with her jewelry in the shoulder pads. In a separate room we women underwent searches by police matrons. Did they really think I would hide gold in my vagina?

The military police picked up all furloughed Jews at the synagogue, to rejoin their forced labor units. It was a last-ditch attempt by the Hungarian government to keep them within the borders. Of course, our men resisted, refusing to abandon their families. The tumult was frightening, but the guns won.

Just before nightfall, we rode, standing up, in an open motorcade to the municipal stables of my hometown. Ági Salgó and her mother rode with us. Paralyzed Professor Salgó was missing. "Papa died last night," Ági whispered. "Suicide."

"I'm so sorry," I squeezed her hand.

"Don't be," she shook her head. "Mama and I let him die."

•   •   •

I spent my nineteenth birthday, July 3, 1944, in the foul odor of the stables. Straw clung to my blue cotton dress as I visited friends and relatives in their horse stalls. They embraced me, saying "Isten éltessen," the Hungarian version of "happy birthday." I had never considered its true meaning, until my boyfriend's sickly mother murmured it like a prayer. "God keep you, Jutka," she embraced me, stealthily wiping a tear. "I won't be at your wedding. Take care of my son."

"I will," I nodded, a promise too lightly given.

We had only a handful of young men with us at the stables, who happened to be on leave from labor service. The handsomest was Dr. Laci D., a dashing physician in his twenties, called "*aranyhalacska—* little goldfish," a name given to the most desirable bachelors in town. To everyone's amazement, just a couple of weeks before, Laci had consented to marry the misshapen daughter of a colleague—pro forma, we assumed. "Don't tell me!" people had snickered. "Why should Sári marry? She is too old for a girls' transport."

Sári was only forty, but seemed a generation behind my mother, with her sallow face and old-fashioned bun. Her family name, Holló— raven, fitted her well. She used to be a neighbor, and I often watched her amble her crooked way along Kontrássy Street, an apparition with eccentric clothes and bizarre shoes.

Sári's and Laci's unexpected mating soon became the talk of the stables. "Have you heard the latest?" Ilona giggled. "Sári Holló and Laci D. are *really* married!"

Just-wed Évi Kárpáti was more explicit. "Sári Holló," she snickered. "That half-mad old spinster. To make love in the stables! Ugh."

There were plenty of witnesses. Our transport, Somogy county's Jewry, was tightly packed—six people to a horse stall, five thousand to the stable. "I've watched them coupling," people reported and others claimed to have identified the sounds. What sounds?—I wanted to ask, but was too embarrassed.

• • •

Soon, we listened to shrieks coming from curtained torture chambers. The Nazis wanted to know where the rich hid their treasures. Bandi Pogány, Ilona's mild-mannered father, shrieked the longest. When the Nazis finally parted the curtains, Mr. Pogány stumbled out, hardly recognizable. His blond hair was disheveled, blue eyes blinded, spectacles shattered, fingers bleeding. The Nazis had shredded his back, his hands, and his feet. But Mr. Pogány had not told them that he had hidden his whole coin collection, the labor of decades, in an unused well.

"Would you believe it, Jutka?" mused Böde Winternitz, a former neighbor of the Pogánys' on Castle Street. "To suffer such torture for mere coins! And Mr. Pogány so sweet, so gentle, always tipping his hat to me, even when I was little. Such an unlikely hero . . ." Böde's round eyes moistened with tears: "Suppose we have to defend ourselves from rape, Jutka? Will we be as courageous?"

"Don't start on that, Böde," I said, impatiently. "I can't stand it. By the way, had you heard the latest? About Sári Holló and Laci D.?"

Böde rewarded me with a shy little smile. "It's true then?"

"It's true all right," I snickered, my eyes on the ill-matched pair. "God bless our honeymooners." What else was there to laugh about?

Workmen coupled cattle cars in front of the stables.

6
ARRIVAL
Kaposvár, Hungary and Auschwitz,
Poland • July 5–July 8, 1944

I DON'T remember much about the loading of the train: all I know is that Ilona's family and mine got separated. I recall the moment the engine pulled us out of the Kaposvár station with an intensity that still hurts.

Our cattle car was packed with seventy-five people. I was crouching on my pack, squeezed between mother and Nana Klein. An SS officer came and closed the door. I heard him bolt it—from the outside. It was dark. The engine gave a sudden tug. "We're leaving," Nana choked. "I can't believe this. We're really leaving."

Where to? I tensed. The train was moving east. Toward the Russian front? I leaned across Nana's and Ica's laps, and they held me tight against the lurching of the wagon as I fitted an eye to a splintered crack. Kaposvár's two-story railroad station glided by. Quickly, I glanced at the upstairs windows. "No one came to see us off," I murmured. "No one."

The white station sign, KAPOSVÁR, glided into view with its familiar black lettering. I shut my eye against it. "Kaposvár," I murmured, recalling childhood journeys. I felt angry and rejected: my home let me go without a farewell. "Mama," I murmured, shocked at my own words, "I never want to see Kaposvár again."

"You can't mean it, Jutka," she sighed. "You can't mean it."

I rode for a long time with lids shut, blocking the tears. When at last I glanced around in the dim light, my eyes were met by a dark gaze, the bride Sári Holló's.

No one in the suffocating cattle car looked more forlorn than our honeymooners. They perched across the aisle—an inch-wide space—a pathetic pair, caged, stifled. Even with his unshaven cheeks, the young husband stayed miraculously debonaire, his beige slacks neatly pressed, his blond hair smoothly parted. Most everyone else soon looked like week-old vegetables; the groom resembled a fresh-plucked pear.

Not so the bride. With her black hair and peaked nose, she mirrored her name—Holló, raven. I was annoyed to find the honeymooners facing me in the wagon. Why couldn't I be with friends? Of course, I was lucky enough to stay with my family, perched between the Vágós and the Kleins. My sweaty arms were glued to mother on the left and to grandmother Klein on the right.

Two fifteen-year-old girls shared the wagon with us, identical twins, with white skin and red hair that blazed even in the dark. "I pity them," I said, but mother sighed: "I pity their mother more."

Two tin pails stood in the middle of the wagon; one for water, the other for a toilet. I held my bladder until evening; Nana Klein held hers longer.

Dr. Gerő and his young family were huddled near us. He was a dentist, his wife a piano teacher. They had two children: Tomi, age eight, and Marika, age six, who was known in Kaposvár as an exceptionally talented young pianist. During the journey, I often sat with Marika on my lap, her blond curls sticky, her childish mouth gaping for air. By the second day, she wanted no more stories or games. "Lack of oxygen and water," her father explained. Marika dozed on my lap, panting and sweating, until the mug came around. One gulp per person per day was our ration for those three and a half days. We had dry food in our rucksacks, but we couldn't move to reach it, and besides, we were too thirsty to eat.

Marika took her gulp of water and sighed with relief. "Take one more, Marika," I urged her in a whisper, "It's all right." Surely, I reasoned, there must be one extra gulp for our youngest.

Marika's blue eyes were filled with reproach. "But Jutka," she said, as if we were playing some game, "it wouldn't be fair." She passed the mug. I took a sip, a moment's ecstasy, and handed it to grandmother Klein.

At night the roles reversed: Marika crept back to her parents, and grandmother Klein pretended that I was a child again—night and day we wished to cradle or be cradled. "Sleep, my little one, sleep," grandmother would murmur, gently pulling my head way down to her shoulder.

As night changed into gloomy morning, our cattle train rumbled along. Old Mr. N., one of grandfather Vágó's former card partners, died. "Lucky for him," sighed grandmother Klein.

Dr. Gerő suggested that we say Kaddish in the wagon. "There might be no funeral," he explained to sobbing Mrs. N. No more funerals, I thought, remembering the two I had attended: O'papa Klein's formal obsequies in a snowstorm, and grandpapa Vágó's lonely rites in summer heat. Remembering my dead grandfathers, I silently congratulated them.

Two neighbors tied the body of Mr. N. to his rucksack with a belt and suspenders, so he would take up no more room than before. I was relieved to be sitting at a distance. Sári Holló was enough of a burden; every time the train lurched, our knees touched and she shrieked as if electrocuted.

As darkness fell, I tried to sleep bent sideways, my spine in agony. If only Nana weren't so short. In her sleep, she would beg: "A bit of soda water! Please, a bit of soda water." As soon as she dozed off, I sat straight, tipping my head forward to avoid the ceiling. When my back felt relieved, I agonized over my knees. I offered Fate a deal: if only I could unbend my knees again, I'd be content. Ambition? Ridiculous. The Sorbonne? Extravagance. Just let me unbend these knees and I'll be modest. Forever.

On my left, mother kept a silent vigil. Her poor arthritic knees, I thought. But only once or twice. The rest of my family vanished. I listened to the churning of the wheels and to the fevered pantings of our honeymooners. "If only this journey would end . . ." I prayed. But to a god I no longer trusted.

The third day dawned. In the half-light, I gaped at Sári. Surrounded by seventy-three people, she was obscenely stripped to a pair of lace pantaloons and a delicately embroidered bodice—the trousseau of a past generation. My young eyes could hardly believe it: under the sweat-soaked chemise, the forty-year-old bride revealed the breasts of a sculpted Aphrodite. But her face was haggard, her pupils dilated. "Hurry, darling," Laci whispered, struggling to pull on her dress. Shrieking, Sári resisted.

"Let her be," cautioned Dr. Gerő, "Let her be. Madness can be catchy." During the day Sári vacillated between lucidity and insanity, but Dr. Gerő assured us she would recover once the journey ended.

Our train sped through potato and rye fields and villages with Polish signs. I watched it through a crack. How far to the Russian front? I wished my geography were better.

As the third day faded into night, I tried to sleep to escape the nightmare. Wisps of images floated disconnected, then merged into a recurring dread.

• • •

Barefoot and naked, I felt myself shivering in a snowy clearing. Above me dark clouds, around me a black forest. The woods were quiet. Yet I knew death was crouching.

I stood on the edge of a fresh-dug ditch, my toes glued to its icy rim. To my left, a line of girls—all nude—with swollen breasts and pregnant bellies.

"I don't belong!" I gasped, wanting to fly away. My arms winged apart, but my toes held to the icy rim. The forest exuded a revolting stench. I was paralyzed by fear.

Suddenly, German troops emerged, their guns protruding. A giant soldier strode behind me, his foul breath odiously close. I ripped my toes from the frozen rim and dove into the pit. Midair, I shrieked, falling, falling.

• • •

I woke. Would I be raped? Buried alive? A girls' transport! How to escape it?

Suddenly, I heard an engine whistle, then the rumble of many trains. Electric lights filtered through the cracks, hitting gaunt faces and blinking eyes. The noise grew frantic as the engine slowed down: rattling, whistling, barking, shouting. It sounded like the East Station at Budapest. Mother smiled, squeezing my hand: "A city, I bet!"

I pushed my eye into a crack: a long cattle train passed us. What was inside those windowless wagons? People? I thought of the Italian Jews who rode through Kaposvár in bolted cattle cars only last year. We could not quite believe it then.

A white station sign glided into view with black gothic lettering. "AUSCHWITZ," I read, turning to the others.

"Auschwitz?" said mother. "I've never heard of it."

The engine crept through the busy station, then chose a lone track ahead. Soon, a second sign crept into view. "AUSCHWITZ-BIRKENAU," I reported.

Our train came to a jolting halt. The journey was over. We idled for a long time at the Birkenau station. Old Mr. S. had a heart attack, or something equally dreadful. Dr. Gerő crawled over to examine him. "Lack of oxygen," he said.

At last, the double doors that had been bolted at the Kaposvár station slid wide open. I felt my lungs swell in ecstasy. But the summer breezes brought a strange aroma. Magda sniffed, leaning forward: "My

God!" she whispered, gazing left. "It smells like burning skin. Like chickens singed of feathers."

I stretched my neck and gasped. Giant flames lapped at the night sky. "A forest fire perhaps?" I guessed.

Magda shook her head. "Gruesome," she muttered to herself.

Gently, aunt Ica embraced Nana, pointing at the opposite direction. "Look, Mama. Street lights. How civilized!"

Two skinny male attendants jumped up into our wagon. They looked alike, in striped pajamas and matching caps. Aghast, Magda pointed at the string of digits over their chests: "Look, they're numbered!"

"Bokanovsky twins," I told her, trying to make her smile. "Sprung from a test tube in the *Brave New World*."

"Robots," she shuddered.

In broken German, the men instructed us to leave our packs behind. "How efficient," mother remarked, but to be on the safe side, I pulled out our toothpaste that hid the gold teeth, and stuck it into my pocket.

The two men grabbed people by the arm pits, and threw them pell-mell down by the tracks. The thin, mechanical arms worked fast. In just a few minutes there was room enough to move about.

My knees in agony, I got up, my back bent by the low ceiling, only grandmother Klein was short enough to stand up. "Don't get separated from us, Jutka," she fretted. "I'm scared for you." Had my prudish grandmother heard about mass rape at the Russian front?

People jumped off at the side as fast as they could; the attendants now unloaded only the old and the invalid. But instead of dropping them straight down as before, they heaved them toward the embankment with an immense effort. I watched, horrified, as they swung dying Mr. S., dead Mr. N., and live Mrs. N. all in the same direction. Sári let out an insane scream as she flew after them.

"Jump, everybody!" called Dr. Gerő, and he leaped, catching his children.

"Magda, quick!" I called, sailing off at the side. "Hand me grandmama."

Too late. Grandmother Vágó hung like a rag doll in the robot's arms. From up high, she addressed him in polite German: "Please, help me down." The mechanical arms stopped in midair, and slowly, gently, the robot placed grandmother down by the tracks. "Danke schön," she said, as if a gentleman had helped her politely out of a carriage.

Magda tossed the others to me. Mother was thin, Nana Klein and aunt Ica child-size; I caught them easily. Then Magda leaped, and our family was on solid ground.

"Goodbye, Jutka," Dr. Gerő embraced me with his free arm. "Avoid a girls' transport. God bless you."

The crowd was streaming toward the railroad station. "Rest a minute," I told my family, "I'll be right back." The earth was heaving under my feet as I elbowed my way through the mob. Did they toss the insane with the dead? I must find out. It will give me a clue to this place, Auschwitz-Birkenau.

At the curbing, between two glaring lights, I found a hill of people, the living and the dead piled like a haystack. The flaming sky framed it all. A funeral pyre!

I searched, nauseated. Was Sári among the dead? Buttocks on faces, heads over jerking feet, necks falling off the edge. At last, I spotted her buckled shoe, still kicking at the bottom. I glanced from Sári's shoe to my sandals; they had been neighbors on the long journey.

I should leave at once, I thought, but the pile held me. I recognized a face: Dr. Margit Nemes, my former professor of French and German. She was buried several bodies deep, shrieking insanely, eyes dilated, mouth foaming. My skin went clammy, my eyes dimmed. I musn't faint! Not here. Not now. An SS guard was approaching. What if he spots me and throws me on the pile? I backed away, swallowing hard. My family! How could I have forgotten them? Dizzy, I pushed my way through the crowd. So much happened in a few seconds, I was trying to sort it out. Dr. Nemes looked insane. Each wagon must have had its share of demented. But why did they pile the old and the insane with the dead? Poor Mrs. N., Sári, Dr. Nemes . . . I mustn't think about them. Was I cruel? I agonized. So be it. Better be cruel than mad. It's a new world, a different planet. I must adjust to it.

At last I spotted my family waving from the tracks. "Where have you been?" mother scolded. "I've been frantic."

"Nearby," I muttered.

"Stay together," she grabbed my hand. "Stay together." It was a command that was to guide us through the months ahead.

Nana Klein blinked her shortsighted eyes: "Where are we, Jutka?"

Aunt Ica took her by the arm. "Come with me, Mama."

Here and there SS soldiers stood guard with baggy breeches and stiff boots. Some held hounds on leash. I shuddered with the primordial fears of childhood.

Ahead of us, a tall SS officer was shouting commands: "To the showers! To the showers!" Families parted readily, men to the left, women to the right. Everybody expected to meet again after the showers.

We queued up, anxious to bathe and drink at last. "Showers," sighed grandmother Klein. "I would have prefered a tub."

"You'll like a shower, Nana," I coaxed her. "It's more hygenic."

Beyond the railroad tracks, once more the line branched in two. Why? What was going on? I slipped ahead to investigate. Under a bright light, an SS officer was conducting a selection. I did not see Ilona, or any of my friends, but I did recognize several women from our wagon. From a distance I watched the selection. Children and older women went to the left, the rest right. Perhaps we girls will be safe, I thought. But the next moment I saw youthful Mrs. Gerő being shoved to the right, away from her children.

I was scared for them, especially for Marika, and I went ahead to listen as a stocky SS woman tried to calm everyone. To each frantic question, she gave a curt but reassuring reply: "Yes, mothers may visit their children. Please understand, women over forty and children under sixteen won't have to work, so they must be separated from the rest. Don't worry, they'll have comfortable quarters. Yes, you may visit each other tomorrow." It all sounded fairly reasonable. I returned to my place in line and naively relayed all that false information word for word.

"The cut-off is forty!" mother panicked. "What to do? What to do?"

"You won't have to work, Mama," I consoled her. "It'll be easier on your arthritis."

The small remnant of our family now reached the parting of the ways. Aunt Ica went first, with Nana Klein. Ica was mother's age. "Left!" signaled the SS officer. Ica did not protest. I watched them walk away arm in arm, my aunt and my grandmother, two diminutive ladies with diminutive steps.

Grandmother Vágó was next, with Magda. In an instant, the SS split them apart. Magda started after her mother, but the SS shoved her rudely to the right. "Stay with the young ones, Magda," said grandmother Vágó. "I'll be all right." And she hobbled on alone, bent and stiff-legged.

Mother and I were next. The SS whisked us apart, but mother hung on, staring into the officer's eyes, as if daring him to separate us. The officer threw her a surprised look. "Wie alt bist du?—How old are you?"

My first reaction was, he talks. And then, it's no use.

Mother lied without a moment's hesitation. "Acht-und-dreissig—thirty-eight." It worked. The SS flung us to the right.

In less than thirty seconds, our family had been cut in half. "Mama," I said, "how did you think to lie?"

"It just came to me."

"You're amazing, Rózsi," Magda allowed, scampering up. "But what about mother? She'll be alone."

"Why do you say alone? She'll be with Ica and Mama Klein." Magda walked on without replying. Mother persisted: "We'll see them tomorrow. After work."

A low cement building appeared ahead of us, all lit up. The flaming sky seemed nearer now, and the smell of burning flesh sharper, but I was too thirsty to pay much attention to it. For a moment I glanced at the stars, happy to recognize the Great Bear to my right. Childishly, I felt safe, walking between my mother and my aunt. But all the way to the showers, Magda kept repeating, "Poor mother. My poor little mother."

7
A Hostile Planet
Auschwitz-Birkenau, Poland • July 1944

WE were led in front of a single-storied, whitewashed building and told to line up for the showers. The spotless anteroom smelled of disinfectant. Reassured, I started to undress at once.

"The Germans *are* hygenic," I remarked to Magda.

"How can you trust them?" she muttered.

I was in my underwear, kicking off my shoes, when an SS woman entered, fully uniformed. "Leave your clothes on top of your shoes," she called. "They'll be easier to find." We piled our clothes into the furthest corner, and quickly I pulled out our toothpaste that held the gold.

"Put it back, put it back," mother hissed. "Can't you see? They take away everything at the door."

Nude and empty-handed, we filed into a brightly lit, windowless room. The door closed. Thirstily, I stared at the shower heads that lined the walls. I grabbed one and stood, face up, waiting for the water to flow. For an instant, I thought of Nana Klein. Would she like the showers?

Then water rained down, cool and soothing. I splashed and drank, totally relaxed.

"Heraus! Heraus!" came the command, and the hall emptied at the opposite door. The large room we entered was whitewashed and bare, filled with striped attendants and naked women. The steamy air stung my nostrils with disinfectant.

A woman in a striped dress grabbed me by the hair and attacked me with scissors. Another drove a razor around my crown. I stood in a heap of my own hair, fingering my scalp; the stubble was foreign to touch.

A shove in the buttocks propelled me along the assembly line. "Raise your arms!" came the command in German. Two females shaved my two armpits in unison. I glanced ahead for mother and Magda. A voice barked: "Spread your legs!" A razor moved into my crotch. A shower of disinfectant hit my armpits and scalp. A sudden spray scorched my vulva. An attendant shoved me from behind. I landed outdoors. Moist air, like the sea, hovered between me and the sun.

I forced myself to look around. Barbed wire fencing hemmed me in on all sides, strung on tall posts that curved in at the top, like question marks—or gallows—rising from the fog. No hills. No trees. No grass. A wasteland of clay and wire. In the distance, weird sentry boxes, bizarre lampposts, identical barracks. The liquid sky stretched infinitely distant—sky of a hostile planet.

Just ahead, a couple of striped attendants were handing out ragged clothes. I got in line, my neck craning for mother and Magda. But the women had vanished. A mob of bald beggars milled about, each marked on the back with a huge, blood-red cross.

I gasped at the shorn prisoners. All men, I thought. And I am naked! My hands flew to my breasts and my crotch. A robot threw me a frayed dress; it was heavily soiled yet reeked of disinfectant. I pulled it on. The loose rags clung to my wet buttocks. A few steps ahead, a pail of crimson paint, reeking of lye. A robot dipped a wide brush and raised it to my back. I cringed, my shoulder blades tensing, as the painted cross scorched through the rags, biting my skin.

A male inmate in a ragged blanket rushed at me with outstretched arms: "Jutka! We thought we had lost you!"

"Is it you, Mama?" I groaned. She wanted to embrace me, but I recoiled. Her pretty face was transformed by the shorn skull: the features stronger, the nose more masculine. Was it a mere hair style that made her feminine?

"Jutka," said mother, glaring at my scalp, "you look like a boy."

Next, Magda appeared. With her bald head and flowery gypsy gown, she looked like a young man in woman's clothes. "You resemble Imre when he had a boy's crew cut," Magda stroked my scalp.

"Let's go!" mother rallied. "We must catch up with the rest of the women."

"Hold hands!" I cried, and we dived into the mob. Arms outstretched, fingers clasped together, we struggled to cut ahead.

Soon, I spotted a familiar face. "From Kaposvár?" I called.

The youngster was preoccupied with a wailing companion. "Évi, Évi!" the older creature sobbed, "What's to become of us?"

"Évi Kárpáti!" I gulped, elbowing near them, "It's you, isn't it."

"Who are you?" she muttered.

The crying woman drowned us: "My God! My God! Why didn't we kill ourselves before!"

"Mrs. Kárpáti, my dear woman," mother scolded. "How can you talk of suicide? Before your own daughter!"

Mrs. Kárpáti stared at Évi's bald head in horror: "My God! My God! And this, your honeymoon!"

The mob soon tore us from the Kárpátis, but mother, Magda, and I held on to each other until we reached a dirt road that ran at right angles to our path. Here, the crowd formed ranks of fives, flanked by SS guards and dogs. Reluctantly, still thinking our shorn comrades males, I fell in line. I hung my head, eyeing dusty bare feet and beggars' rags: not even my toes looked familiar.

Distraught, I looked around. To my left, tall sentry posts, high barbed wire fences. Flat, grassy fields beyond. To my right, low, brick barracks on a clay terrain. The haze was lifting, and I stretched out an arm to bask in the sun. All might be well, I thought, all might be well after all.

With pounding boots, a couple of SS guards passed us. The elder, a robust man, pointed beyond, at a block of doorless, windowless barracks. They were wood, unpainted, with unfinished roofs. "Siehst du? Das ist ein Vernichtungslager."

Vernichtung, my mind reeled. But that means making something into nothing. Annihilation! An annihilation camp? Impossible. I must have misunderstood. But the young guard repeated in unmistakable German: "Vernichtungslager! Really? And we're taking this crowd there?"

"Jawohl," replied the older. "To Birkenau. Lager B III."

• • •

July 1944, Auschwitz-Birkenau, Lager B III. Our barracks were unfinished, because there was no room for us elsewhere. Inmates of surrounding barracks named it "Mexico"—the poorest of the poor. We, its inmates, wore rags instead of striped prisoners' garb, sipped soup brewed of twigs and leaves, and suffered the blazing sun without drinking water. No one was meant to survive there for more than three weeks. And no one did.

Without bunks, each half-built barrack held five hundred. No room to lie down. At night, we slept on the dirt floor, sitting cross-legged or lying on someone else's buttocks. The weak dozed, standing up, pushed against the walls. (Decades later, I was to recognize similar conditions in a chicken coop.)

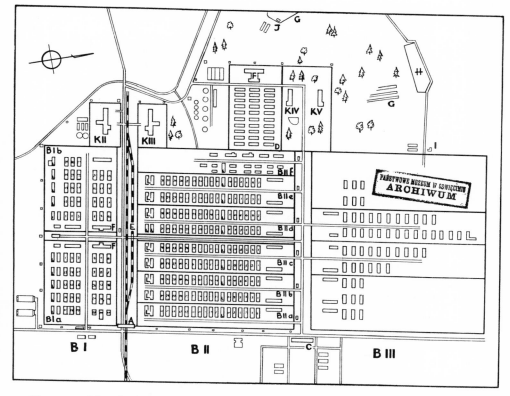

The map of Auschwitz-Birkenau (1944). We stayed at the barracks B III, described as "Mexico" by other inmates.

KL Auschwitz II (Birkenau)

A   main guardhouse with watchtower
BI   camp sector I
BII   camp sector II
BIII   camp sector III (under construction)
BIa   the women's camp
BIb   originally a men's camp, from 1943 a women's camp
BIIa   quarantine camp
BIIb   family camp for Jews from Terezin (Theresienstadt)
BIIc   camp for Jews from Hungary
BIId   men's camp
BIIe   Gypsy camp (Zigeunerlager)
BIIf   hospital for prisoners
C   camp HQ and SS barracks

D   warehouse containing the possessions of murdered victims ("Canada")
E   the ramp on which incoming transports were unloaded and selections made
F, G   pyres on which bodies were burned
H   mass graves of Soviet POWs
I   first provisional gas chamber
KII   gas chamber and Crematorium II
KIII   gas chamber and Crematorium III
KIV   gas chamber and Crematorium IV
KV   gas chamber and Crematorium V
L   latrines and washrooms
Arabic numerals indicate huts in which prisoners lived

Zähl Appell at Auschwitz-Birkenau. Bald-headed Hungarian Jewish women as photographed by the SS. From the *Auschwitz Album* by Lili Mayer. Courtesy of Yad Vashem, the Holocaust Museum in Jerusalem.

During the day, we lined up for *Zähl Appell*—head count—and stood in rows of fives for hours and hours. Those who collapsed were trucked away. Between head counts, we tried to sleep.

Night and day, I had a recurring dream.

• • •

Sweating under my dunyha, I woke on Kontrássy Street. The faucet was dripping only a few yards away. "Water!"—I rejoiced and ran where the bathroom would be. Water trickled, then cascaded, cool and soothing. I bent to the sink and opened my mouth to it. I gulped, ecstatically.

• • •

On an especially hot day at noon, as I woke from this dream still gasping from thirst, I found myself outside on the bare ground. I couldn't see my mother anywhere in the crowd. "Magda!" I shook my aunt, my voice barely audible. "Where is Mama?" She pointed at the hunchbacked beggar sitting at my toes—his bald head was bouncing up and down, his white tongue hung loosely between cracked lips.

I pulled myself up to my knees and squinted into the haze. Thousands upon thousands of bald heads covered the flat terrain as far as eye could see—mushrooms wilting on the parched soil. "Magda," I moaned, "Mama's gone." The hunched lump stirred at my feet and a familiar, graceful hand clasped mine. "It's I, Jutka. It's I."

I held the long fingers with the familiar nails—pink, rounded shells, elongated and pearly. "Sleep, Mama," I whispered. "Go back to sleep." And gently I cradled her bald head in my lap.

• • •

For two days, mother, Magda, and I clung together, never letting each other out of sight. We stood *Zähl Appell* in the same row of fives. Together, we walked to the latrines, our fingers clasped, our arms extended, our legs stepping over the sprawling crowd. At the open latrines, I held my nose. One behind the other, we lined up for the same foul hole, afraid of being separated.

"Where does it all come from?" I marveled as I urinated. We had had nothing to drink since the showers at arrival.

By mid-morning, mother passed out again. Magda and I dragged her into the shade of the barracks. "Please, Sir," I begged, in my confusion still taking my comrades for males, "please, make room for my mother." A couple of bald figures shifted until Magda and I wedged my mother's head between their buttocks.

As I sat down again, I noticed a handsome girl asleep, her shoulders leaning against the barrack, her skirt hitched up, her nude thighs spread to the sun. She was smeared with thick blood, some of it still flowing, most of it caked. The messy paste covered her shaven crotch, trickling along the inner thighs. She must have been flowing for days. Her bunched-up skirt was soaking it up—a loathsome bandage. That's what we are, I shuddered, under the clean clothes and modest panties, that's what I have been.

The crowd of bald prisoners dozed, oblivious to the obscenity. What if they should awake? We are surrounded by men! I must remind that girl to close her legs. If only she were nearer . . . But wouldn't she just fall asleep, and her sticky thighs spread?

"Magda," I whispered. "Are you asleep?"

"What is it?" she murmured.

"Look," I said, pointing at the menstruating girl. "I want to puke. When is yours due?"

"I can't remember."

"Me, neither. Suppose it's soon. What then? If only we had some cloth or paper."

"Don't worry," she said, closing her eyes again. "We won't last until then."

Our talk was suddenly interrupted by the arrival of the water wagon, a drum on two wheels, drawn by a couple of slave girls. Magda and I picked up some messy, discarded mugs.

"Water! Water for my mother!" I heard my voice, like a beggar child's. Was this Jutka Magyar from Kaposvár? Magda and I trailed the drum, vainly trying to catch some drops.

The haze was lifting, the sun nearing its zenith. Mother slept on, pale and panting. She'd faint again soon. I turned to Magda in a panic: "This place is a Sahara. Without any oases. We'll all get sunstroke. I'm suffocating!"

"Sleep," Magda muttered. "Sleep, if you can."

I put my palms over my scalp to shield it, but I felt too hot to sleep. My eyes fell on a gap in the mob ahead of us—a kidney-shaped puddle about twenty feet long. "I'll be right back," I told Magda. "Don't move away from here." I gathered myself up and dragged myself over. Bending to the surface, I waited for the dizziness to pass.

The rim was crowded: half-naked creatures crouched on all sides. Some knelt down to dip their scalps, some cupped their hands to slurp it. Magdolna Frank (her maiden name) of Kaposvár was washing her swollen breasts, her eyes dazed, her scalp welted. I recognized her by her almond shaped eyes. She had given birth not long ago, I remembered. Where was her baby?

I gazed at the shallow water. Slimy and stagnant. Urine? Vomit? The stench was horrid. My fingers ruffled the yellowish liquid. It was cooling. I sprinkled my scalp and bent down, cupping my hands again. Should I drink it?

A small figure drew near: blond crown, childish face, yellow-green eyes: "Jutka!"

I let the water dribble from my hands. "Ilona," I said, "I took you for a boy."

As we did in Kaposvár, we touched fingertips. "What did they do to your ears, Jutka?"

I felt them with my hands. "They stick out a bit, they always have."

We giggled for an instant, relieved to be together. "I recognized you at once, Jutka," Ilona said. "A dress helps, I guess." She wore a tattered, faded-blue shirt that barely covered her privates. No skirt.

"You'll be more tanned than I," I tried to make her smile.

"We aren't at the Balaton, Jutka. Were you going to drink from the puddle? It's poison."

"What of it?" I shrugged. "D'you know what this place is called? *Vernichtungslager* —annihilation camp."

"Annihilation?" Ilona repeated. "It figures. One can't survive without water. But there's a way out, Jutka." She turned to point at the barbed wire fence not fifty feet away. "Shall we?" she asked, as if suggesting a stroll. "What d'you think?"

I thought of the puddle and the loathsome sight of the menstruating girl. "The electric fence," I nodded. "It'll be fast and clean. Let's go." A former me listened, mystified. Were we deciding on suicide, Ilona and I?

Hand in hand, we took a few steps toward the fence, but I stopped, feeling guilty. "I'm with mama and Magda," I muttered. "And you?"

"Mother and aunt Vilma went left. I'm with Évi, Zsuzsi Schwarzenberg, and her mother."

"Shouldn't we tell them about the electric fence?"

"I suppose so. I'll bring them tomorrow. You won't drink from the puddle til then?"

"Of course not." I felt alert, almost vivacious; something to do, something to plan. "See you tomorrow, after first Zähl Appell."

I watched, as Ilona's small, erect back receded into the crowd—bearing the painted cross.

•   •   •

Ilona did not come to the puddle the next day, or the next. I thought she had changed her mind about the electric barbed wire fence. Magda warned me it would be a horrible death; she was for hanging ourselves, instead. "I'll make a rope out of my gypsy dress," she offered. "We'll take turns." But nothing came of it. We were too lethargic.

By the end of our first week at Birkenau, we regained our senses. Often, we'd talk of home, of family and friends. "When shall we see the grandmothers and Ica?" I wondered.

"Never," Magda whispered.

"What d'you mean?"

"Nothing," she groaned. "I didn't mean it."

"Of course not," mother soothed. "We must be patient."

• • •

Soon, we had no more trouble recognizing each other, and I dared go to the latrines alone. One morning, as I was standing in line for a crowded hole, I noticed a couple of girls with hair the length of bristles on a brush. "You girls must have been here for quite a while," I said.

"Three weeks," answered the redhead, but the brunette corrected her: "It'll be three weeks tomorrow."

"Three weeks!" I marveled. "I didn't know anyone could survive here that long. Where're you girls from?"

They named their village in Transylvania.

I told them I was from Trans-Danubia, from Kaposvár.

"From Kaposvár!" they cried, excitedly. "Your men were stationed near our village."

"*Our* men?" I exclaimed. "Who? When?"

"They may still be there for all we know," smiled the brunette. "We last saw them a couple of months ago in the ghetto. Whom d'you want to know about?"

I named my father, uncles, and my boyfriend.

"Peti Hanák!" guffawed the redhead. "You must be his girlfriend, Jutka."

"How do you know my name?"

"From Hanák's poems," jeered the redhead.

I blushed, embarrassed. I thought Peti's poems too intimate; how could he have shared them with these strangers? Quickly, I changed the subject: "You girls have been here for three weeks. How did you manage?"

The red head swallowed involuntarily as she eyed the hunk of bread in my hand. "We've been eating our rations—not like you dumb Trans-Danubians."

"But it tastes like sawdust," I shuddered. "My throat is so parched, I can't get it down. I was just about to throw it into the latrines."

"Really?" gasped the redhead, greedily grabbing it from my hand.

"Give back her bread," ordered the brunette. "How could you take it from Peti's girlfriend?"

"D'you speak Yiddish?" the redhead eyed me quizzically.

"I understand it some," I hesitated. "I speak German."

"Some Jew!" she sputtered. "Worse than the *goyem*."

"You two are off the subject," the brunette interrupted as she transferred the hunk of bread back to my hand. "Hold onto it, Jutka. Drink your soup, and you'll be able to swallow your bread. It's that simple. You need the liquid."

"The soup makes me puke," I protested. "It's nothing but twigs and leaves."

"Dumb *Mamelander*," sputtered the redhead. "You pampered weaklings of the homeland, you'll starve to death here." It was her turn on the hole, and shrugging contemptuously, she mounted it without another word to me.

"I'm next," sighed the brunette with relief as she took a small step ahead. "Remember, Jutka," she turned back to me, "if you ever see your poet again, tell him how you met us at the latrines in Auschwitz-Birkenau. And listen to me, don't be so damn finicky. Hold your nose and drink your soup. It's the only way to survive here. Farewell, it's my turn to piss."

At noon, I noticed that some of our comrades were swallowing their soup. Mother, Magda, and I closed our eyes, and eventually, we got down some of it.

• • •

A few nights later, as I was dozing cross-legged on the dirt floor of our barrack, a drop landed on my shorn scalp. "What's this? I mumbled, waking. I parted my lips and offered my tongue to it. "Rain!" I cried. "Mama! Magda! It's raining!" Gratefully, we sucked in the rain as it splashed in at the doorless entrance and seeped through the unfinished roof.

Refreshed, we slept, but puddles soon formed. I woke, finding myself sitting in muddy water. I scampered up, and so did some four hundred roommates. The searchlights revealed a sorry lot: wet limbs, drenched rags, bald heads as slimy as fishes. At last, a sharp whistle called us to the ill-lit courtyard. We ambled out to the "kapos'" bilingual curses. The Germans rarely came to Lager B III-b, we were left in the charge of a "kapo," an inmate bribed with extra rations to do the Germans' bidding. Ours was a sadistic Polish woman who was fast with the whip. She had been incarcerated for years. According to Birkenau legend, she had fought with the underground and lost her husband and children to the Germans. But pity did not temper our hate.

In addition to their longer hair, barrack bosses were recognizable by their yellow arm bands. But not our female Goliath. She wore a canary yellow blouse as if her ample arm had been transformed into a gigantic torso. We called her Yellow Blouse—kapo extraordinaire. She was assisted by a Hungarian Jewish girl, who was elevated to the post by means of the whip and arm band.

Predawn *Zähl Appell* was never an easy task for the kapos—too many prisoners fainted out of the ranks—but a predawn head count during our second week was the worst that I recall.

An icy rain lashed viciously in the dark, and it chased mother, Magda, and me from the edge of the phalanx; the more the kapos lashed, the more everyone shoved toward center. I could see how panic mounted at each sweep of the searchlights.

Shivering uncontrollably, I wedged myself deep into the midst of the crowd. This is it!—I sighed, my pores sucking in body warmth. This is it, the primordial embrace of the tribe. I had a sense of déja vu—felt rather than seen. Had predecessors hardly human huddled for warmth like this?

By noon, the truck had carted away more than the day's portion of dead, then the sick were made to undress, and to crawl nude into the emptied vehicle. Magda and I held mother up by the armpits, so she would be allowed to stay.

Afterward, the kapos counted our reduced ranks, then let us disperse at last. Mother, Magda, and I stretched out on the muddy ground, still side by side. The wind had stopped, the rain was warm and soothing. I fell asleep at once.

Was it hours or was it minutes? All I know that I woke to singing—liquid echo to rain:

> Fölöttem sír az ég,
> Sírnak a fellegek,
> Álmaimban mindig haza járok,
> Várnak reám akik szeretnek . . .

> Above me weeps the sky,
> Darkly, the bleak clouds roam,
> Dreaming, I wing, I fly,
> My loved ones are waiting at home . . .

"Above me weeps the sky," I hummed with my comrades, and for the first time since our arrival the tears came. Afterwards, I sang full-throated if slightly off-key. The kapos stood by without trying to stop us—the Rain Song was stronger than they.

It isn't exactly a Bartók-Kodály composition, I smiled to myself, recalling music professor Lendvai's discriminating tastes, but neither is this a March Fifteenth Festival at the girls' gimnazium.

No music had ever moved me more. Perhaps it was the size of the all-female choir—several thousand strong—perhaps it was the contrast of setting to music. Was the anonymous songster still alive, still huddling here? I glanced at the bald, ragged chorus, trying to guess who our composer might be. Suddenly, I felt more awe than I ever felt for Béla Bartók or Zoltán Kodály. "My loved ones are waiting at home," I sang with my comrades, and I began to fantasize about my boyfriend.

The heavy rain soon brought a marked change. During our third week in Auschwitz-Birkenau, bread became an obsession instead of water. Some devoured it, some munched it by morsels. Mother, Magda, and I divided our daily hunk into three bites: for morning, noon, and night. It felt civilized.

Besides recalling Socrates, I often found myself humming Beethoven's *Ode to Joy,* or repeating my favorite lines by Ady: "Aki él, as mind, örüljön, / Mert az élet mindenkinek / kivételes, szent örömül jön—Life is a gift, sacred and choice / All who live / Rejoice, rejoice."

Everybody talked of home now—mostly of recipes and men. But what if the men should return before us? We wanted to cover our nakedness, and unlike Eve in the Garden of Eden, we had to include our nude heads. The going rate for a ragged kerchief soon rose to a day's ration of bread. My family was spared the cost: Magda's gypsy gown sufficed for two, and I ripped a band from the hem of my dress. No one would call me "sonny boy" anymore.

Someone had found a needle, and I decided to borrow it. Reluctantly, I broke off a small piece of bread to pay her fee. Why do I bother?—I asked myself, as I hemmed my kerchief with some unraveled thread. We women were a strange sex, I decided: we sustain our sanity with mere trifles. Even in hell. Yes, even in hell.

It was now easier to recognize friends; I met several, among them Ági Salgó and Böde Winternitz. Ági wore nothing but an apron. "Look at this, Jutka," she turned around, to show me the crimson cross painted on her skin. "My father was right to commit suicide. Wasn't he?"

"And a good thing you let him," I nodded, reassuringly.

Ragged Böde Winternitz seemed to have more courage here

than during Adam's Apple's history class. "We'll make it, Jutka," Böde squeezed my hand. "Won't we?"

•   •   •

A day or two later, as I was ambling my way from the latrines, I noticed a familiar face with a proud chin and bushy, dark eyebrows. "Jutka Magyar!" she grabbed my hand.

"Szervusz—Hi," I muttered.

"You don't recognize me," she grieved. "No one does. I used to see you at the Pogánys; Ilona and I were classmates."

"Your name?" I murmured.

"Bondi Kasza," she blushed.

"No! It can't be!" The Kaszas were a prominent Protestant family in Kaposvár.

"It seems that my maternal grandparents were born Jewish. Mother came too, but she went left. I'm alone."

"And your father?"

"Papa is Aryan, of course. He must be fighting at the side of the Germans. Ironic, isn't it?"

"Does he know about you?" I asked, feeling unexplainable pity.

"I doubt it."

"When did you find out about all this?"

"Just as the gendarmes came to drag us to the station. They didn't give us time to pack, the beasts."

I glanced at my dress, as ragged as her own. "It doesn't make much difference, does it?" Quickly, I changed the subject: "Have you seen Ilona Pogány?"

"She was taken to the hospital with her sister and with your mutual friend, Zsuzsi Schwarzenberg."

"Ilona, Évi, and Zsuzsi? All three at the same time?"

"Scarlet fever. There's an epidemic. I'm immune. Have you had it too?"

"Yes, as a kid," I nodded, remembering. "As a matter of fact, I had been playing with Ilona, Évi, and Zsuzsi just before coming down with the rash, but none of them caught it."

"More is the pity," Bondi sighed. "By the way, Mrs. Schwarzenberg went with them. The kapo let her."

"That's good," I nodded, unaware of the gas chambers.

The whistle for afternoon head count interrupted our talk, and we parted with a hasty farewell. The sun was hot and Yellow Blouse out of temper. Face contorted, she chased her young assistant back into the ranks. Reviewing our blocks contemptuously, she raised her whip and pointed me out: "You! In the brown dress. Step out."

Trembling, I stepped in front of the thousand. Why me? What did she want?

The kapo roared in her Slavic German: "Donkey! Do you speak German?"

"Jawohl, Kapo," I cringed.

The interview was over. Next moment, I was transformed into the kapo's assistant, complete with a whip and a canary yellow arm band.

"Line up, you swine!" Yellow Blouse bellowed, and I rendered it into polite Hungarian: "Please, girls! Line up by fives." It worked. My comrades obeyed me without the lash.

After the head count, I ran to my family: "We'll get double the bread, and plenty of water—all three of us!"

"To think she picked you out of a thousand," mother embraced me. "Wait til I tell papa!"

At sundown, Yellow Blouse kept her promise, handing me six rations, a mug of water and a nearly new blanket. "Don't let the swine push you off. You're kapo for the night." I watched, my back to our barrack, as she strode into the darkened camp with an insane laughter.

I handed my whip and my blanket to my family : "I'll join you later." From the doorless entrance I viewed the scene: the pecking order was in full force, the strong stretched out, the zombies leaned against the walls, the majority dozed, cross-legged, on the clay floor. Suddenly, I noticed three women sleeping on their sides, heads on each others' buttocks, feet on each others' calves. They fitted like spoons in a drawer.

Eureka! Gingerly tiptoeing between thighs and arms, I rearranged my comrades onto their sides. I felt a high, such as I had never experienced before. My idea will spread the length and breadth of Auschwitz-Birkenau!

Unfortunately, there was a minor flaw in my plan: before I had a chance to bed down the entire barrack, the strong stretched out again, the weak leaned against the walls, while the majority sat up hunched and cross-legged, as I used to do.

"You've been up all night, Jutka," mother scolded me as we met at the door.

I felt exhausted and defeated, and couldn't manage to herd my columns into fives.

"Use your whip, you cursed donkey!" Yellow Bouse bellowed at me during a sweep of the searchlights.

"Jawohl, Kapo," I lied.

"I can't see you! Come here!" I ran.

Yanking a tall girl from the front row, Yellow Blouse motioned to her bright red kerchief. "Rip it off, you bitch, and put it on yourself!" she roared at me, raising her whip. I felt immobilized. "Rip it off, you stinking idiot! Or back to the lines you go."

I dropped my whip, ripped off my arm band, and fled, wedging myself between mother and Magda. "I'm sorry," I apologized.

They hugged me, putting their arms about my shoulder: "We'll make it, Jutka," mother smiled encouragingly.

Without the whip, I felt free. "I'm going for a walk," I announced after the head count.

"Where would you go?" mother fretted.

I glanced around: barbed wire fence, puddle, barracks, latrines. "I'll investigate Lagers 'c' or 'd,' " I said, and took off for the unfinished barracks behind our own.

Along the way, I met a novel sight: a pair of spectacles perched on an inmate. I approached the elflike creature dressed in a petticoat. With her small, shapely breasts and bald head, she looked part girl, part boy. "You kept your glasses!" I laughed. "That's amazing!"

"Not really," she flashed a leprechaun smile. "I wore them in the showers." She tore off her lenses and grinned at me, squinting. "See? I'm blind without them." With spectacles back on her tiny nose, she eyed me, gaily: "Where're you from?"

"From Kaposvár."

"I'm Éva Jámbor," she introduced herself. "From Zalalövő."

I reciprocated by giving my name—a rare exchange in Birkenau. We sat down on the dry clay and struck up a conversation, my first since I arrived here nearly three weeks ago. It turned out that we were nearly the same age, and both planning to study comparative literature after the war. "The mind reels!" laughed Éva, finger to her forehead. "We'll be in the same class at the University of Budapest."

"How about Paris? Have you thought of the Sorbonne?"

She leaped to her feet like a ballet dancer. "I'd love to discuss it some more, Jutka," she smiled. "But not now. I must run. My mother'll be worried."

"Mine too," I chuckled. "This is beginning to sound like at home. Will you visit me next? At Lager III b, by the Puddle."

"Listen, Jutka, I've got an idea!"

"You don't say," I grinned. "Idea" was not a word one heard at Birkenau.

"I'm serious. It's Friday, and there is a Mrs. Paskusz leading Sabbath prayers by the Puddle."

"The mind reels," I mimicked her. "Sabbath prayers at Birkenau?"

"She's been in touch with the underground."

"I can't believe it! But I'll come. Why not? When does she start?"

"Sometime before last *Zähl Appell*."

"See you then."

•   •   •

"Which of these creatures would our famous Mrs. Paskusz be?" I asked Éva as we met late that afternoon.

She pointed at a mob forming within the mob: "That must be her circle." A short woman stood at its center, surrounded by a group of young girls. "I'm Lea Paskusz," she introduced herself as we edged near her. "This is my daughter, Kornélia." Mother and daughter resembled each other, both short, with olive skin and flashing black eyes—Kornélia's delicate beauty contrasting with her mother's leathery look. Mrs. Paskusz had a prayer book in her hand, and she pulled out two candle stubs from the folds of her blanket. "Sorry, no matches," she apologized as she placed the candles on her young daughter's outstretched palms—a living candelabra.

"Where did you get the prayer book and candles, Mrs. Paskusz?" Éva asked.

She smiled mysteriously: "I've got my sources."

Mrs. Paskusz's Sabbath prayers started with "L'ho Dowdi," the introductory song familiar to me from childhood. Recalling Friday night services with O'papa Klein, I wiped a tear. "Mustn't wax sentimental," I whispered to Éva.

After prayers, Mrs. Paskusz turned into war reporter, briefly recounting the latest Allied advances on both fronts.

"How d'you know all this, Mrs. Paskusz?" asked a pert voice.

"I've got my sources," she repeated. She bid us spread the news, then blessed us in Hebrew with hands extended: "The Lord bless thee, and keep thee. The Lord make his face to shine upon thee and be gracious unto thee. The Lord turn his face unto thee, and give thee peace."

"Amen," we murmured.

Mrs. Paskusz suggested that we come nightly from now on. A few days later, she bid us tighten our circle, then pulled out a wrinkled scrap from the folds of her blanket. "Pass it around. Quickly!"

I trembled with excitement as I held a quite recent clipping from a German newspaper, dated July 22. The article reported on an attempt made on Hitler's life by his own generals.

"Who gave it to you, Mrs. Paskusz?" Évi marveled. "Someone from the underground?"

"Shhh . . ." she cautioned. "Never refer to them." Her sermon was short and to the point: "We've suffered like Job, girls. Please God, it may soon be over."

"Amen," we chorused.

"Will you come again tomorrow, Mrs. Paskusz?" asked a timid voice.

"If we're still here."

"*If*, Mrs. Paskusz?" Éva was quick to note.

"All of Lager B III will be emptied as soon as we're tattooed. Bless you. Bless you all."

Next morning, mother, Magda and I watched the tattooing at La-ger B III a. "It doesn't seem to hurt much," I said, watching a slave burn a number into a girl's white wrist under SS supervision—point by point, digit by digit.

"The poor girl will be disfigured for life," sighed mother.

"Don't worry, Mama," I said, reading her thoughts, "I'll catch a husband regardless."

As it turned out, the SS never got around to tattooing our barrack. Early next afternoon Yellow Blouse called us to an extraordinary head count.

8
STAY TOGETHER!
Auschwitz-Birkenau, Poland • July 1944

THE sun was in the west when the kapo, Yellow Blouse, finished the head count. But she wouldn't let us disperse. "Single file!" she roared in her Slavic German, "Single file, you swine! Single file!" We milled about, confused. In three weeks at Auschwitz-Birkenau, we had never stood *Zähl Appell* except by fives. Red Kerchief, the assistant kapo, danced her own whip above the heads of the crowd. "C'mon, girls!" she coaxed in Hungarian, "Forget the fives!"

A telling froth bubbled from Yellow Blouse's mouth. She swooped at her young assistant. "Whip them, you devil," she croaked, "or I'll whip you to a pulp!"

I watched, hypnotized. The events of a few days ago flashed through my mind. Suppose I had not resigned as a kapo? I'd be wearing that red kerchief now. My successor raised her whip and shut her eyes. "Don't!" I wanted to shriek. But Red Kerchief struck. Once. Twice. Then again. "Damn it all," swore a comrade, "We've got another rotten kapo now."

Both kapos lashed until all of us—the entire Lager B III b— queued up into a long, twisting line. "Attention, swine!" Yellow Blouse bellowed. "Off with the rags! Medical exam."

Medical exam? My hands flew to the front of my dress. Where is the doctor? The mob buzzed, a frantic beehive. Buzzed, but hardly moved.

"Off with those rags!" echoed Red Kerchief, whipping at bare shoulders and scalps. I pulled off my dress quickly.

Mother shed her blanket and stood nude and frail in front of me.

"Both kapos have gone raving mad," she whispered. "I'd die if you were one of them."

But I am not—I boasted silently to Socrates and Dr. Biczó.

Magda leaned forward to whisper: "Another selection? What d'you think, Jutka?"

Red Kerchief rushed by, whipping with closed eyes: "Line up, you scum!" she shrieked, striking out at random. I winced, mortified.

"March!" barked the kapos in two languages and one voice. And we marched in a gigantic curve around and around, naked.

I was nauseated by all the nudity, the breasts, the buttocks, the pathetic pubic slits, so visible on the shaven parts. I stretched my neck to see beyond our own compound: grey earth, pale sky, thousands upon thousands of bald women swirling in the nude. Twenty-first-century Europe? The Brave New World is dwarfed by comparison—the same mad discipline, the same infernal crowding, but our world beastly, Huxley's overrefined.

A sharp whistle brought me back to the moment. Yellow Blouse yelled: "Up with the arms! March, left!"

Left? Which way was my left now? The kapos herded us with shouts and lashes. We filed out of our own compound and started, naked, down the main road between the barracks.

Glancing around, I tried to estimate the size of the crowd. Thirty or more barracks . . . each barrack now down to three or four hundred: some ten to fourteen thousand nude women! Who would believe it? After the war, they would have to make a movie, a Hollywood epic—Budapest wouldn't have the props. I gazed at the scene to record every detail, more like a spectator than a participant.

My arms ached from holding the dress up high, and the tender skin around the nipples blistered in the sun. But amazement muted all pain. I was still bewildered by all the nudity, especially my own, and I blushed hotly when a male figure came into view. It was an SS officer, in full military attire, complete with hat, jacket, white gloves, and tie. Surrounded by thousands of nude women, he looked bored as he fingered his pistol.

I shall call him Dr. Mengele, because of what I've read of his role, and because several of my former comrades recognized him later from his photo. But personally, I did not think to study his features and I cannot be sure.

My attention was completely absorbed by a hound and a tall kapo who held it fast at Mengele's side. Of the group of three, man, woman, and beast, I, naively, dreaded the beast. As the nude women filed past, the hound was tugging at the leash, trying to lick the bleeding parts.

Mengele put away his pistol and began brandishing his cane. The swish of his staff parted the row of nude women into three distinct herds. He sent the majority straight ahead, toward the freight train. The sick and worn wobbled left, toward a waiting truck. A select group of young girls steered right and marched off nude, in rows of fives.

Mother glanced back, pale under her white-fuzzed scalp. "Don't worry, Jutka. We'll be off to work camps."

I whispered to Magda with lips rather than sound: "Mother is optimistic."

"Isn't she always?" Magda replied.

Ahead of us, the mob was reassembling along the railroad banking. Some of the women were still naked, others were pulling their rags back on. "See, Magda," I pointed, "no kapos. They're staying behind. Just lucky, I resigned."

"Lucky? Have you looked left and right?"

To my right, the block of young girls was marching off in the nude. A girls' transport for the Russian front? My uncle Imre's warnings came again: "Risk your life to avoid a girls' transport."

I searched for familiar figures among my would-be comrades. I thought I recognized two: a girl from our barrack and my former classmate, Ági Salgó. Frantically, I signaled to Ági, but she did not turn around; her tight twin buttocks floated away on the sea of the naked. Imre's dread image rose again—the pregnant girls, the ditch, the shots.

Magda touched my arm, pointing to the left. The discarded wobbled along, stooped and skeletal. Mechanically, a couple of striped attendants heaved the nude wretches on a waiting truck. The women on the bottom, could they breath? Could they breath at all? The scene on arrival came again: Sári, Dr. Nemes, the pile; I shuddered with a sudden insight into our options. Straight ahead—slave labor. To the left—death. To the right—mass rape at the Russian front.

"Magda," my voice broke, pleading. "We'll go straight ahead, won't we, Magda?"

"Can't you see?" she whispered, pointing to the right: "It's the girls' transport for us."

"Magda! But you're married!"

"It won't matter to the soldiers."

"And mother?"

Magda whispered close into my ear: "I'm terrified. Your mother is five years beyond the Nazi deadline. And her new hair has come in so white."

"Mama," I anguished, leaning forward, "let me . . ." I pulled down the blanket to cover her white scalp.

"Quick!" hissed Magda, "Tell her not to walk so stooped."

"Mama," I whispered, "pull back your shoulders."

"I will, I will."

Mengele swung his staff, randomly but rythmically, as he let the majority of the mob stream ahead, toward the freight train. But he shoved every fourth or fifth woman left or right. Five more women remained in front of us now. Selfishly, I hoped the SS would send at least one of them left or right, but Mengele's cane swept all five toward the freight train. God, my God! Mother'll go left!

Mengele's gaze fell on my nude torso, while his cane whisked mother routinely ahead. I did not have a moment to rejoice. "Rechts!" snapped Mengele, his cane at my breasts. "Rechts!"

Was it the terror of rape that emboldened me, or was it the hope of staying with my mother? Perhaps it was only a surge of adrenalin. I forgot I was naked. I forgot Mengele's gun. Ignoring his command, I started after mother. The hound growled, the kapo pushed me to the right with a tone of well-meant advice: "Go with the young ones. Run!"

"I'm going with my mother!" I said, and turned back again.

"Bitch," she yelled, roughly now. "He'll shoot you down!"

"Let him," I said, suddenly calm. "I don't care." Once more I turned and followed mother, this time slowly, with deliberate steps. How easy it is to face death, I thought. In the middle of my back, a tiny spot began to tingle, expecting the bullet. The spot seared into my flesh. I glanced over my shoulder: Magda was sprinting after me, her nude thighs leaping high.

"She's my mother too!" Magda lied in fright. How beautiful she is, I thought, strangely detached.

The Kapo yelled: "Fools! He'll shoot you both!"

Mengele lifted his pistol. My eyes shut themselves. Was the gun pointed at my aunt's naked back? "Magda, run!" I cried, and we fled until we reached the thick of the crowd. I glanced back over my shoulder. Mengele's right hand was on his pistol, the left one swung the cane—ahead, ahead, fast. A statuesque blonde was next in line; Mengele's cane swept her—right. That luckless girl, I mourned, and Ági Salgó too. But my racing heart beat its own triumph: all those others, but not Magda . . . a whole transport, but not I!

In the west, a red sun was sinking fast. Mother caught up with us, panting hard. "You're here! Both here, with me!" She let the blanket drop on the ground and sank on it, naked. Knees clasped in tight-knit fingers, she rocked herself, slowly, rythmically, like a cradle. "I'm so happy! So happy! I've never been so happy in my whole life!"

9

ALONE WITH
THE KOMMANDANT

Hessisch Lichtenau,
Germany • August 1944

ONCE more the train. No food, no water. Without the packs, there was room enough to lie down, and we all curled up, pillowed on each other's buttocks.

A day or two later, we landed in the small German town of Hessisch Lichtenau; I don't know the exact date, for we had lost count. At Lichtenau, we became laborers, cogs in the Wehrmacht, fillers of grenades. We lived in former German workers' barracks in the village, and we worked shifts at the munitions factory in nearby Fürstenhagen, an enormous underground plant which we reached by two long walks and a train ride. There, we helped to manufacture shells. Officially, we went by numbers assigned by the SS: mine was 561.20578, mother's 561.20579, Magda's 719.20713.

Since we had so recently come from Auschwitz-Birkenau, we marveled at the people in the village. They lived in houses, among trees, behind lace curtains. We had spent only three weeks at Auschwitz, but we had forgotten this other Europe, this other twentieth century.

Every day, before we left for the factory, and again on coming back from the Lager, we lined up for *Zähl Appell*. At Auschwitz, *Zähl Appell* was a senseless, Kafkaesque torture, interminable hours of agonized huddling; here, they simply counted our heads, from one to one thousand.

As I stood at *Zähl Appell* on that sunny afternoon, I dreamed of

Our former barracks in Hessisch Lichtenau. Photo taken shortly after the war. Courtesy of Professor Dieter Vaupel.

Paris and the Sorbonne; I'd study there, I hoped, by fall. I stood barefoot, in a drab, shapeless dress, but my dreaming head was capped by an azure kerchief, winged and magical.

I was enormously proud of that bit of sky-blue cloth, having outwitted the whole Lager system for it: I pilfered it at the weapons factory out of a bin of wiping rags, I sneaked it back to the Lager hidden under my blouse, I hemmed it with a needle I begged off a comrade and I washed it in ersatz coffee I stole at the risk of my life. Lathered in hot coffee, rinsed in cold water, and pressed by my palm, my kerchief emerged, radiant. True, it was nothing but a swatch of torn mattress cover, but I had gambled my life for it and won.

I stood at *Zähl Appell* on that fateful afternoon, with my bald head capped in azure—as if Maeterlinck's bluebird of happiness had perched on my shorn crown. Not even Marika Erdős's Hungarian headdress had made me prouder.

To my left—close enough to touch—the electric barbed wire fence; to my right, rows upon rows of unpainted barracks. A soft breeze brought the scent of grass—there had been no grass at Auschwitz—and with it that line from Ady: "Aki él, az mind, mind örüljön—all who live, rejoice, rejoice."

Facing us, with the barracks for a background, stood the Kommandant and the kapo. I glanced at them, amused that they resembled each other: both blond, blue-eyed, lean, and wide-shouldered. At another time, they might have been lovers, but of course, the very idea was laughable. The Lager's Kommandant, Kommandoführer Wilhelm Schäfer, was an SS officer, sworn to destroy us, and the kapo—though temporarily serving the Germans—was one of us, a Hungarian Jewish captive.

Manci Pál, the kapo, was handsome with her high cheekbones and flashing teeth. "I bet Manci left a boyfriend behind," I thought, and began to fantasize about my own.

Suddenly, I realized that the Kommandant had departed from his usual script as he turned to Manci: "Suchen Sie mir ein sauberes Mädchen—Find me a clean girl."

Would he use us for his harem? I agonized. The Kommandant's face was impassive; I watched Manci's for clues. The kapo blushed, and a nervous twitch fluttered one eyelid. Her sisters and friends stood in the front row, ready to grab the best jobs, but Manci's glance avoided them. Clearly, the kapo was searching for a victim. Whom will she choose?—I wondered, relieved to be standing in the back. I stretched my neck in all directions: hundreds and hundreds of young faces, each framed by a drab kerchief. Poor Manci, what an awesome task . . .

"Hurry!" barked the Kommandant.

Manci's eyes swept the heads. "You!" she pointed me out. "You, in the blue kerchief."

I have no memory of the next few moments; I must have become mentally paralyzed. Did the Kommandant call me from the ranks? Did I give my mother a desperate parting glance? I must have come to my senses just as the gate opened to let me out—me and the SS Kommandant. Desperately, I craved the anonymity of the crowd, the protection of the fives, the guards, the hounds. The irony of it!—I thought.

The Kommandant strode ahead in his stiff breeches and pounding boots. Instinctively, I followed, my head cast down, my eyes on the graveled road. I had a flash of recognition, as if I had followed a past master in such dumb obedience. Do women inherit memories of rape?

I recalled the myth of the Sabine women and the tale of Hunor and Magor and their abducted mates, the legendary ancestors of Huns and Magyars. "My plight is not unique," I told myself, "I'm caught in an ancient rite of sex and war."

As I followed the Kommandant through the village, I wondered what the inhabitants of Lichtenau thought of us: a slave girl stamped with a huge red cross following her armed master. Did the burghers of Lichtenau feel pity for me? It was a civilized little town, neat and peaceful as Kaposvár had been. Women nodded to each other "Grüss Gott," as they met on the sidewalks. But they averted their eyes from me.

From time to time, the Kommandant glanced back as if checking on his shadow. I walked some ten paces behind him, keeping it constant. Only once did I lag for a moment—by a mountain ash brilliant in the setting sun. If only I could turn into a tree . . . I feared rape, and I wondered what intercourse might mean in physical terms. The girls' gimnazium had censored our reading, and my sex education derived from a handful of post-Victorian novels.

I now tried to recall a favorite scene from Hemingway's *For Whom the Bell Tolls*: the hero and heroine making love in a sleeping bag. But another scene kept interfering: the rape scene at the barbershop.

I had read Thomas Mann's *Joseph and His Brothers*, and I began to fantasize about winning the Kommandant's trust. Even as a child, I was intrigued by the tales of triumphant slaves: Joseph as Pharaoh's confidant; the Greeks introducing arts and religion to the Romans. But male slaves were no models! What if I should become pregnant? "D'you know, Jutka," my mother had hinted a thousand times, "you were born *exactly* nine months to the date of my wedding." A boast and a warning at the same time. My vanquisher's breeches puffed out at each stride: nine months from today, I might give birth to his bastard.

Closing my eyes, I saw us scuffle on a couch. Should I beg him to kill me? How do I say it in German? "Bitte, töten. Bitte, töten mir." I mustn't panic. There must be a way out.

Of course, there was and always will be a way for captured women to avert death: by becoming concubines. I ruminated about the lot of all the women captured in all the wars, in every inhabited spot on this planet. The Sabine and the Magor mothers were famous models, but similar dramas must have unfolded millions of times. I could hear Mr. Kőváry's lecture: "The enemy raped and plundered, they slaughtered the men and took all the women and children hostage." Of course, it was always the enemy who committed those detestable acts. Never one's own nation. Never one's own tribe.

What became of all those abducted women? Why hadn't I identified with them before? The majority must have been enslaved or murdered. But some, like the Sabine and Magor women, became trusted mates. For women, submission was the safest tactic. The only tactic?

I tried to project myself into the role of a concubine: sexy, docile. Vainly, I conjured up some simple scenes: baring my breasts, helping the Kommandant with his bath. What do a man's genitals look like?

The Kommandant's shadow was blending into dusk, and I railed at the sun for abandoning me to my fate. No more dreaming and fantasizing! Not some mythical figure but I, Jutka Magyar, would be raped tonight.

I became alert, wrought up, like before an exam. I must have a plan. I knew I had one advantage, I spoke German well. My grandfather Klein, a devoted teacher, had instructed me until the day he died. I had been thirteen, but already familiar with the classics. For an instant, I could hear my grandfather's elderly voice reciting my favorite poem: Schiller's *Die Bürgschaft*.

"What d'you think of this, O'papa?" I wanted to ask him. "Here I am in Germany at last, but not to study literature. Would you have believed this? What should I do? What should I do?" If grandfather were here, he'd speak for me. And the Kommandant would listen; people always listened to O'papa.

My other grandfather came to mind, the baker, Vágó. "Don't be afraid to speak to any man," he had told us in the ghetto. "They all had a mother, same as you and me."

Quickly I thought of a possible scenario. I could pretend that I had venereal desease. "Syphilis," I'll call it, the name must be the same in German. We had studied some of the symptoms, because the disease had killed Ady, a foremost Hungarian poet. But Dr. Biczó had discussed it psychologically, not medically. Could syphilis be detected on the genitals? Would the Kommandant examine me? I projected the scene in horror.

With trembling fingers, I uncovered my dizzy head. The azure-blue kerchief floated limp in my hand. Why had I stolen that bit of ill-fated cloth? Why did I wash and press and sew it? Only to embellish my naive head. What silly vanity. I touched the moist, stiff bristles. Perhaps my boyish look would move him to pity. But dare I count on such a meager strategy?

We had reached the opposite end of the village, and I had still not found a viable plan. Should I plead for his pity? The Kommandant was an officer, and naively, I expected him to be an educated man. He might also be sentimental. Germans often were, even the cruel ones. I recalled the heroes of grandmother Klein's German romances: fierce and daring, but instantly moved to pity by the plight of women. "Lemonades," my grandfather had dubbed her books, and he banished them from the living room. Those heroes of hers were surely exaggerated, but wasn't an SS Kommandant an exaggerated character also? Just this past week, I managed to defy one of them at gunpoint. Do I dare take the risk again? I must—unless I find another way out.

I recalled my studies in German, in psychology. I made up one opening sentence, then another. The mental effort reminded me of my preparations for the baccalaureate exams only the summer before. I tried to think of the best words, the most-apt German expressions. I wished I had a dictionary. My first sentence must have the power to reach his soul. If he had one. But that was my only hope, the chance I was gambling on.

It was dark when the Kommandant turned off the road. He swung open the gate, strode up the path, and bid me follow. My heart pounded, as it had never pounded before, not before any exam, not before any danger. What shall I say the moment I cross the threshold?

By supreme willpower, I restrained my racing heart. Like an actress stepping on the stage, I stepped into the lighted house.

10
OPTIONS
Hessisch Lichtenau,
Germany • Autumn 1944

"**W**AIT here," the Kommandant ordered, wiping his feet on the cocoa mat by the entry. He switched on the light, locked the door, and strode abruptly across the floor. Stunned, I watched his broad back advance into another room and disappear behind a closed door.

My eyes darted across the parquet floor—identical to ours on Kontrássy Street—and skittered desperately, instinctively around the anteroom. A wood-paneled coatrack, like grandmother Klein's, framed a full-sized mirror. A massive bureau loomed under an unwound clock. A windowless beige wall bore family photographs and blank, faded rectangles where pictures had been removed. The SS must have sent the occupants packing in a hurry.

I clenched my fists and dug my nails into my palms as a cabaret tune sprang from a gramophone beyond the door. What was he doing? Taking off his clothes? Slipping into pajamas? Drinking schnapps to the sound of sexy music? A drunken SS. Could I fight him off?

The door to my right was open a crack, revealing a pool of electric light. I tiptoed over and peeked in. Lace curtains hung in front of black-out blinds. Twin beds pushed snugly side by side were decked with white puffy pillows and a pink summer quilt.

Face flaming, I backed away, and caught my image in the mirror. Bowlegged from badly trampled heels, my shoes torn, my dress spattered with machine oil, my head pathetically shorn, I looked like a slave. Taking advantage of a mirror, I tied on the azure kerchief: I won't face him bald. I'll appear as a civilized woman, not the anonymous slave he takes me for.

A young woman suddenly appeared behind me in the mirror. I gaped at the contrast: platformed white sandals; silk stockings; a print dress with padded shoulders; bouffant hair-do; a piquant face with heavy makeup. The Kommandant's mistress! I must be safe . . .

"Here you are," she said in a lower-class German accent, and pointed at my filthy rags with a grimace. "Are you the clean girl we were suppose to get? Never mind. We'll soon get rid of your dress."

Get rid of my dress? Haven't I escaped yet? Kaposvár gossip came to mind—a young bachelor in our neighborhood was rumored to have carried on an affair with two people simultaneously—a man and his wife. Did the Kommandant's mistress have a ménage à trois in store for me?

"Wait a minute," she said, and striding awkwardly on her platformed sandals, she disappeared into the kitchen. Scared, I returned to the cocoa mat at the entrance, just where the Kommandant had left me.

The music came to a halt as someone lifted the needle. In the silence that followed, the Kommandant boomed from the bedroom: "What's keeping you, Liebchen?"

"I must instruct the girl," answered his mistress, entering from the kitchen.

Instruct me?—I shuddered.

In her outstretched hand she held a wooden brush with natural bristles and an elastic strap on the back. She handed it to me. What for—I shivered. "Do you know how to polish parquet floors?" she said.

But of course! She just wanted me for a scrubwoman. A clean girl to clean house. How simple. How amazing.

Tears of relief gave way to instant tension. New strategies were needed at once. "Gnädige Frau—gracious lady," I ventured, "I have never cared for such elegant floors before. Will you teach me how?"

"Sure," she smiled condescendingly. "One more minute, Liebchen," she cajoled, stepping to the bedroom door. "I must give some instructions to my cleaning woman. Wait for me, darling. I'll be right back." The Kommandant's mistress hurriedly introduced me to the mysteries of floor maintenance, and I studied it with zeal. Soon she hastened to the bedroom, leaving me blissfully alone.

Humming a csárdás, I washed, waxed, and polished the parquet floors, my left foot skating on the soft brush, my right foot dancing on lamb's wool. Suddenly, I noticed a pincushion on top of a bureau, an embroidered stuffed cotton heart. I skated over to count the needles.

Eight. I pulled out a medium-sized one and held it between two fingers, examining it greedily. Back at camp, it would purchase a choice of valuables. A day's ration of bread, or three carrots, a quarter of a cabbage, two raw potatoes, a bar of soap—the possibilities were endless. Seven or eight? It wouldn't make any difference to her . . .

I felt no pangs of conscience, no moral scruples, only the dread of becoming a thieving cleaning woman—the kind we all despised at my childhood home. Hesitantly, I stuck the needle back into the cushion and resumed my footwork over the parquet—feeling superior.

Long after midnight, a flushed brunette appeared in a revealing negligee. Inspecting the floors, she approved: "I couldn't have done it any better myself." She picked up a bottle of aspirin from a bureau drawer and popped a couple of tablets.

Mother came to my mind with her aching right elbow. Dare I say anything? "My mother used to take aspirin for her arthritis," I ventured. "Our infirmary doesn't have any. They've got nothing, nothing at all."

"You've got a mother?" she said, surprised, and quickly spilled the leftover pills into my palm. "It's too bad about the infirmary. But don't blame the Kommandant; he's only following orders from above."

Afterwards, she sent me to the kitchen to scrub an iron pot with chunks of meat and potatoes left on the bottom. I gobbled them up. My fortunes were rising, my stomach cheered.

When the Kommandant reappeared, he was wearing his officer's hat and white gloves. "Good-bye, my love," he smiled, squeezing his mistress with a uniformed arm. "I'll bring the girl tomorrow. In a clean dress, I promise." A clean dress!—I silently rejoiced.

"Wait a minute, Willy." She stepped to the icebox and pulled out a gold-rimmed white china platter with a slice of lemon meringue pie on it. "Hold out your hands," she bid, and slid the pie on my spread palms. I was ecstatic: I had landed the best job at Lichtenau Lager! How proud mother will be.

As I followed the Kommandant through the sleeping village, I held my pie tenderly, winking at the moon for witnessing my success. The pine forests delivered their pungent aroma from the distance, reminding me of father's tales of childhood in the Carpathians. After the war, we would visit there, he had promised us.

Mother and Magda came running to the gate, followed by Manci. "All's well!" I burst out laughing as soon as I entered. "The Kommandant just wanted a 'clean girl' to clean house. Imagine that!"

Mother held me tightly: "I prayed and I prayed . . ."

"We've been pacing camp for hours and hours," said Magda, and pointing at the kapo, she added with emphasis: "None of us slept."

Manci nodded her assent. I had guessed right, I inferred; the kapo had picked me for a victim.

The next sweep of the searchlights illuminated my prize, the slice of lemon pie oozing from my fingers. "Wow!" cried Manci, her eyes narrowing with greed. "Pie, no less!" To my annoyance, mother handed her a generous bite. Manci licked her fingers: "Mmm . . . Delicious! What else did you get to eat, kid?"

"Meat," I told her, naively. "Potatoes and meat."

"Meat!" marveled Manci.

The next day I was shipped back to the factory. Manci's bosom friend Klára[1] became cleaning woman to the Kommandant's mistress. The kapo used me as a trial balloon, I fumed, a dummy to test the course. To my newly made friends I made light of the incident, but inwardly I held a grudge against Manci, averting my face whenever we met.

"Let bygones be bygones, Jutka," mother warned me. "No use fighting authority. We can't afford it." Hoping to appease Manci, who seemed to have noticed my disdain, mother devised a scheme. She borrowed a pair of scissors from the camp seamstress and stole them to the factory under her dress. Knowing the punishment would be losing her newly grown hair, she stealthily cut off a strip from her rubber apron. Back at camp, she fashioned three stylish roses: one for the head seamstress, one for the chief cook, one for the kapo. The seamstress took it as her just due, having lent the scissors and the needle, but our big-bosomed cook was pleased. She dipped her ladle deep into the pot for all three of us that evening, fishing out plenty of potatoes and turnips. "Here," she said in her gruff tone. "Eat."

Manci, the kapo, waxed emotional as she accepted mother's gift. "I don't deserve this." She blushed, adding, "You're a real lady, Mrs. Magyar." Amazed that Manci knew our name, I tried, but could not bring myself, to forgive her: Klára waxed fat, working for the Kommandant's mistress, while I continued to slave at the factory.

• • •

We, one thousand Hungarian Jewish women, were the only concentration camp prisoners assigned to this factory, and we wore blue-and-white triangular emblems to designate our inferior status.

On my return to the factory, I was assigned to pulling heavy wagons loaded with filled shells, and the Germans ordered me about as "Pferd—horse." Mother and Magda had anonymous jobs, they lifted shells like almost everyone else.

---

1. I wasn't able to confirm her name.

Early in October, Magda had a stroke of luck: she was assigned to machine-stamp shells with initials and identification numbers. But one evening her luck turned to misfortune. At the beginning of night shift, the foreman stepped behind her back, shouting: "Mach schnell! schneller!—Hurry up! Faster!" He threatened to switch her and her partner, Ibi, from the best job to the most dreaded: filling shells with vaporous poison. Ibi panicked and pushed down the foot pedal too fast.

The heavy iron plate landed on Magda's finger. I heard the shriek from the next room and rushed over with my wagon. Magda was on the cement floor in a half-swoon, cradling her left hand as she repeated over and over; "No, no, no . . ." I glanced at her left hand and felt nauseated; her little finger was gone; only crushed bone and flesh mingled with blood and machine oil remained.

"I'll find mother," I told Magda, and ran, abandoning my wagon.

Mother came, leaving her place by the moving belt without permission. When she saw Magda, she kept calm. "She's my daughter," she told the foreman. "Please, find her a doctor."

The foreman found the supervisor, who brought his superior. The incident was fully investigated and recorded, but nothing was done for Magda, who was left bleeding on the cement floor. A guard chased mother and me back to work at gunpoint, swearing unintelligibly. The supervisor moved Magda's trembling partner, Ibi, to fill shells with poison.

Magda joined us some seven hours later for the three-hour trek back to camp: a long walk to the Fürstenhagen railroad station; an endless wait in rows of fives for the train; an excruciating ride to Lichtenau standing up; a last weary trudge from station to Lager—our twice-daily routine that left us scant time to do more than sleep. By the time we arrived, Magda was corpse-white and shaking uncontrollably.

The female SS guard we called "Hyena" dragged her to the infirmary, which was staffed by three woman prisoners with medical training who had been brought from Auschwitz: two nurses and a young Italian Jewish doctor, Luciana Nissim. A little, dark-haired woman with flashing eyes, Luciana saved lives without medication and fought the SS for each prisoner she excused from work.

Luciana inspected Magda's hand and shook her head disconsolately: "I haven't got the tools to treat this," she mourned, "all I can do is wash it."

Hyena said she'd send her back soon, but first she took Magda to report the accident to the Kommandant. Mother and I followed. The Kommandant was shaving in his shirtsleeves by a window of his barrack, one cheek foamy with soapsuds. He glanced at Magda while

Hyena made her report, then returned to his shaving without a word. "Please, Kommandant!" mother cried out.

"What's up, prisoner?" he stopped the razor in midair.

Mother held up Magda's crushed stump covered with dried blood and machine oil. "My daughter needs medical care," she asserted. "The infirmary has no bandages, no disinfectant. Please, Kommandant!"

"The Russian doctor will come Friday as usual," the Kommandant assured her.

But mother stood her ground. "Today is only Tuesday. Have pity, Kommandant! My daughter is a victim of the German war effort."

"I'll be damned," mocked the Kommandant, "a heroine, no less." But to everyone's amazement, he bid a guard escort Magda to the village doctor.

"I'm going along," mother announced, striding after them. Pretending not to notice, the Kommandant returned to his shaving.

In the physician's waiting room several people rose to offer their seats to Magda, mother told me afterwards, but a stern look from the SS guard made them sit down again. The crushed finger was amputated and the stump carefully bandaged. In the privacy of the doctor's office, his wife slipped a small apple into Magda's pocket—an object of marvel when it appeared in our barrack.

As the stump healed, Magda became a *Lager Arbeiter*—camp worker, assigned to clear tables in the dining hall with her good hand. The group was a minor aristocracy at camp—just under the cooks and seamstresses—who slept in a barrack of their own. In addition to the handicapped, it consisted of the kapo's former neighbors and friends.

During an afternoon *Zähl Appell* in late October, the Kommandant pulled a sheet of paper from his pocket. "I've got an important announcement," he said. We listened, transfixed. What could it be? "A message from headquarters," he pronounced. "Two hundred prisoners are needed at a nearby camp. For easier work. Anyone over thirty-five or disabled may volunteer." And he added, threateningly: "No malingerers!" Manci translated.

We returned to our barracks to confer on mother's cot. What should we do? We had half an hour to decide.

Mother was for leaving. "I won't last another month lifting those shells," she sighed. Then, turning to Magda, she blushed like a girl: "We might meet Jani or Feri. Or Peti," she added, glancing at me. I tried to conjure Peti's blond image, but it eluded me.

"You're a dreamer, Rózsi," Magda whispered, "but I'd like to believe it."

"I'm sorry to disappoint you both," I said, "but the Kommandant will never let me leave. Only you two are eligible."

"That's just it," mother said excitedly. "Don't you see? Magda lost a finger, which makes two eligible—a majority. Misfortune turned to luck! Don't worry, Jutka, we'll stay together. The Kommandant will not separate us, I know how to talk to him. It's just as papa said: men listen."

Magda clutched her bandaged stump with the other hand; she suffered from spasms of phantom pain as if the crushed finger were still there. "I feel pretty safe here," she whispered, her face ashen, "but I'm willing to go. You two decide."

"What d'you say, Jutka?" mother turned to me.

Silently, I weighed our options. My instinct told me to stay. The food was scarce but sufficient for survival. My work as "horse" arduous but bearable. Magda was well off as a Lager worker. "You do need easier work, Mama," I allowed, thinking of her arthritis, "but what if they ship us back to Auschwitz?"

"It's possible, yes . . ." mother nodded. "But not likely, Jutka. The Kommandant sounded sincere. Besides, I'm not the only one in danger here. What if they assign you to fill shells? The SS are using Jewish girls for that. You've seen them—saffron to the eyeballs. The poison may never come off . . . It might attack the heart and lungs. I'm scared for you too, Jutka."

The kapo's whistle interrupted our debate. "Maybe you're right, Mama," I murmured, rising from the cot. "Let's go."

And so it was that we volunteered for the death camps. We weren't the only ones fooled. On that overcast day in late September, over three hundred prisoners signed up for two hundred places—including my friend Éva Jámbor with her mother and Mrs. Rózsi Karpelesz from Kaposvár with her daughter, Julia.

The Kommandant appeared as it started to drizzle. "Everybody line up by fives!" he roared. The selection was chaotic. The Kommandant stood by with a bored expression, while Manci did the weeding. "Malingerer!" the flushed kapo scolded in a falsetto as she pulled out some protesting woman. "Too lazy to work here? Get out of my sight."

Reaching our row, Manci turned to the Kommandant, feigning anger: "These three are top-notch factory workers."

"What about her hand?" the Kommandant frowned at Magda's bandage. "Isn't she a *Lager Arbeiter* ?"

"Her hand will soon heal," said Manci. "They're tough women. I know them."

Mother started to protest in German, but Manci switched to

Hungarian, her ice-blue eyes hypnotic: "Grab your daughters, Mrs. Magyar. Run!"

Stunned, mother obeyed.

Our barrackmates greeted us warmly: "You're back! What about Mrs. Jámbor and Éva?"

"The selection is still going on," Magda told them. "It's hard to tell what's happening."

Soon, the three of us curled up on mother's straw mattress to talk things over in a hushed tone. "Why did Manci pull us out, d'you suppose?" I mused.

"I think she meant well," mother considered, chin in hand. "She's been real decent to me since I made her a black rose."

"To me too," Magda added. "She even calls me by my first name since I've become a Lager worker."

"I don't trust her," I said emphatically. "She played me foul before."

"Perhaps she wants to make amends, Jutka," mother tried to calm me. "She must have had a bad conscience since she made a guinea pig of you. She meant well by keeping us together, anyhow. Besides," mother continued, chin in hand, "that transport may well be doomed."

"Have we both changed our minds, Mama?" I pondered. "You seem to think the transport might go to Auschwitz, and I don't anymore. Besides, we all assume that Manci knows the ropes. I wonder what she'll decide about the Jámbors—she likes them real well, I know.

An hour or so later, Éva Jámbor, her mother, and I watched from the barrack door as the group trudged through the gate in a heavy rain. Yellow Ibi—who had been filling shells since Magda's accident—was among them, and so was Mrs. Rózsa Karpelesz and her daughter. I counted them carefully: they numbered two hundred and six, but Manci had pulled out all her favorites. Might all these women be doomed? Shaken by doubts, I turned to Éva Jámbor in a whisper: "How much does the kapo know, d'you suppose?"

She wrinkled her tiny nose. "More than us," she replied. "Less than the Kommandant."

II

SEED OF SARAH
Hessisch Lichtenau and Weimar,
Germany • 1944–1945

A^T Lichtenau, we held no prayer meetings, except during the high
holy days. We fasted on Yom Kippur for the prescribed twenty-
four hours, but fasting had become a way of life, so we hardly noticed
it. "Whether I stay Jewish or not, I shall always fast on Yom Kippur," I
told mother. "I must remind myself that people go without food day
after day."

"A fine resolution, Jutka," she nodded. "But what do you mean, *if*
you stay Jewish?"

"Nothing, really . . ." I shrugged it off, but I had been fantasizing
about emigrating to Australia, where I would marry a gentile. Why in-
flict persecution on my descendants? In my more sober moments I
stayed loyal to my faith and to my boyfriend, but my fantasies conjured
up strangers: Australians, Dutchmen, Frenchmen—men I had never
met, or had met only once or twice. Despite the ban, I talked to forced
laborers who had come from all over Europe, and that lent substance
to my dreams. I recall one such man vividly.

I met him on a warm October night, following a solo stroll under
the stars. Just a few minutes before, as I was dragging my wagonful of
shells, blaming the night shift for my underground confinement, an SS
guard had called: "Horse, come here!"

"Jawohl," I jumped, abandoning my wagon.

"You speak both German and French," he grumbled.

It sounded like an accusation. Had he spied me talking to Frenchmen and Dutchmen? I hung my head, scared. What might the punishment be?

"Ich spreche ein bischen—I speak a little," I muttered.

I needn't have worried, for he only wanted a translator. In monosyllabic German, he instructed me to take a piece of broken machinery to be repaired by a Belgian mechanic. The shop lay aboveground, some half a kilometer away, and to my amazement, the guard chose not to accompany me.

Slipping the small machine into my pocket, I found myself miraculously alone—to think, to feel, to dance. The underground weapons factory vanished from sight; hidden under a forested hill, its camouflage was suddenly perfect. The pine forests exhaled their intoxicating aroma. Humming an air from *The Magic Flute,* I spread my arms: the warm breezes might lift me above the trees.

At the brightly lit machine shop, I was met by a glamorous sight: three charming young men in Gallic berets rushing to meet me. Their melodious French propelled me a year ahead in time: by September, I might be a student in Paris.

My contact, a dark-haired, bright-eyed Belgian mechanic, was a former engineering student. Chivalrously, he shouted his compliments above the roar of drills and grinders. When he spotted my shorn hair under the kerchief, he exclaimed indignantly: "How could they do this to you, Mademoiselle? Brute Germans. We Belgians are civilized." In crisp French, he gave me the news: the list of cities bombed, the list of cities taken by Allied forces.

I envied him his radio: "How lucky you are to be a forced laborer, instead of a prisoner of war."

"You, a prisoner of war, Mademoiselle?" he exlaimed. "The Germans are insane." He shut off the grinder and shifted his voice to a low register: "Did I tell you before?" he smiled, handing me my machine. "You look heavenly in your azure kerchief. Come again! Come again, Mademoiselle."

"If only it were up to me," I sighed, half in love with this handsome stranger. I clutched my repaired machine, return ticket for the journey. "Au revoir! Au revoir, Monsieur."

Outdoors, the sky had been lit by stars; among the constellations I recognized an old friend, Ursa Major, unchanged and intimate. I had last met him in Auschwitz and remembered him well from childhood, stretched over our roof like dog over threshold.

Paganly, I prayed to him: "Take me home, Great Bear, since you know the way."

But he only blinked, knowing much, saying nothing, old sphinx of the night.

For the next few months, I fantasized about my Gallic acquaintance. Autumn was a tolerable season for most of us, although despite Luciana Nissim's valiant efforts five of our comrades died.

In October our daily rations increased and our nightly soup thickened, even yielding an occasional cube of meat. Before long, some of us got back our periods. The SS even issued cloth sanitary pads, and we laundered them in the unheated lavatory, feeling feminine.

As cold weather set in, we received much-needed clothes, and footwear too, to replace our ruined shoes. The guards handed to each of us two sets of flannel underwear, a used dress, a worn, light coat, and—to our intense relief—a pair of Dutch wooden shoes. It helped us celebrate the approaching holidays.

There were no candles for Chanukah, but we sang the traditional melodies and exchanged some fabulous recipes—committing them to memory.

•   •   •

For New Year's Eve, our barrack planned a private party, inviting only my aunt Magda, who continued to room with the camp aristocracy: sweepers and vegetable peelers. Dainty, spectacled Éva Jámbor, whom I had first met at Birkenau, introduced my family to this barrack as soon as we arrived at Lichtenau. I thought it extremely fortunate: many of our barrackmates were Éva's acquaintances, and we all got along well, except swarthy, snub-nosed Marcsa,[1] who had stumbled into our midst accidentally.

"Let's have open-face sandwiches for New Year's Eve!" Éva Jámbor now suggested, and we applauded her enthusiastically.

"Why are you always applauding Éva?" Marcsa shrugged her shoulders. "What else could we plan? Roast goose with dumplings?"

On the evening of December 31, we all crowded around the long table, our coats buttoned up against the cold, our faces scrubbed, our hair freshly rinsed in ersatz coffee, our lips crimson. Enterprising Trudi, a young kindergarten teacher, had found a red crayon stump and passed it around in lieu of lipstick.

Just before the party, we had decorated our rounds of bread with stolen vegetables and paltry lunch rations saved for a week. I thought mine exquisite: cutouts of coppery carrots on cottage cheese, dabs of ruby jam over margarine, slivers of bologna dotted with white turnip.

"We kept ours all in yellow," Mrs. Weiss announced with a sad smile, as she displayed two slices of margarined bread with carrots; her fifteen-year-old daughter, Mici, a delicate youngster with transpar-

1. Not her real name.

ent skin, had gobbled up their decorations. "The poor child keeps growing and growing," Mrs. Weiss sighed, placing an arm about Mici. "Look how bony she has become."

We all relished our sandwiches—each her own. It never occurred to us to share food with anyone but family, not even with Gabi Dénes, a fourteen-year-old El Greco beauty with enormous black eyes who was everyone's favorite.

We had fine entertainment at our New Year's Eve party. Mrs. Weiss, a former dramatic actress, vanished into her bunk and soon emerged with her short hair disarrayed and her wide-set eyes outlined in red crayon. Pacing the tightly packed upper bunks for a stage, she gave us a grand performance of *Macbeth*.

Her rendering of crazed Lady Macbeth inspired pity in us for mad Rózsa,[2] who had been sent away a couple of weeks before to the hospital—we were told.

Rózsa used to be our bogeywoman: nightly she haunted our latrines. During the day, she raved and cursed, tramping the camp in urine-soaked rags, but during the night she slept on a latrine seat. On moonless nights we were terrified of sinking our bared bottoms into her odious lap.

"What d'you think caused Rózsa's madness?" mused Edit, a former gimnazium teacher, who managed to look scholarly with her prematurely white hair.

"Must be a delayed reaction from Auschwitz," Trudi suggested. "Let's hope we escape it."

Freckled Vera quickly changed the subject. "Enough of this, girls! It's New Year's Eve! Year of our liberation. How about some sexy French *chansons*?" We cheered her expectantly, and Vera crooned in her seductive alto "J'attendrais toujours," our favorite.

Mrs. Weiss blurted out between two songs: "I must tell you something, girls," she confided half in jest, "I just realize what a perfect life I led: a fine home, a loving husband, and my daughter well-fed." Cupping her chin into her palm, she glanced at her emaciated Mici, as she added wistfully: "Whom should I have envied, but myself?"

After Vera's performance, my comrades dispersed to their bunks. I turned up my coat collar and slipped out to the silent campyard; every other minute, the searchlights cut off my view of the stars, illuminating the rows upon rows of dreary barracks. Leaning against a wall, I shut my eyes. Where should I spend next New Year's Eve? In Paris, Budapest, Sydney, or Kaposvár?

---

2. I haven't been able to confirm three names: Rózsa, Vera, Edit.

Vera interrupted my revery. Grabbing my arm, she led me to the Kommandant's whitewashed barrack: "Want to hear something amazing, Jutka?"

"A radio program?"

"Oh, no," Vera grinned. "You'll hear some real live music—the finest for the New Year!" Placing our ears to the windowpane, we listened to the SS Kommandant's drunken sobs.

Our report was greeted with glee by our barrackmates: "The SS must be scared to death of 1945! Hurray! Hurray!"

"Let's have a fast *csárdás* in our wooden shoes," Évi Jámbor sailed from her bunk, and while our elders sang and clapped, we hopped the traditional midnight *csárdás*—on the tabletop.

Only one young girl stayed in her bunk, Meda Dános, whom we all admired for her serene beauty. Meda chatted softly with her mother, a handsome woman who seemed refined even in her rags.

• • •

I wasn't as pretty as Meda, but my looks still caused me distress. A week or two into January, as I was splashing myself stark naked in the unheated barrack, in stepped Oberscharführer Ernst Zorbach, trailed by Manci. Zorbach was a homely man in his forties with close-set eyes and a massive nose, who enjoyed kicking women in the rump. Dare I show my back? Dare I show my front?

Mother sprang to shield me from view, her arms spread out, protectively.

"What've we got here?" sneered Zorbach, "A female gorilla guarding her young? A runt, no doubt."

"Haha," blurted the kapo to my anguish, "the girl could model for a Venus."

"Let me see her!" leered the SS, taking a step forward. Next moment, he turned abruptly on his heels and marched out, followed by Manci. Would he fetch me at night? He did not.

January was a frantic month. Food became dangerously scarce, the soup watery, the luncheon rations erratic. Once more we lost our periods. For weeks our only nourishment was a near-empty soup and a hunk of bread. Puci—Margit Dukesz—our tall, gaunt barrack head, handled our only knife with great ceremony as she sliced each small loaf into three equal parts—forty pairs of eyes watching anxiously. Puci never played favorites—in sharp contrast to Cook, who ladled our nightly soup unfairly, some with potatoes, some without, causing needless anxiety.

Before winter was half over, we noticed a shocking contrast between our bony selves and the fleshiness of Manci and her court. How

I envied their undulating hips, especially Klára's. She had become indispensable to the Kommandant's mistress and now managed a large staff of household slaves: cooks, beauticians, dressmakers, cleaning women. As for me, I continued to work in the munitions factory and to starve with everyone else.

No more reveries of sex. Instead, we succumbed to food fantasies. "Guess what I dreamt last night," said homely, good-natured Trudi, who slept in the upper bunk to my right. We were perched in our coats, gingerly wrapping our feet in grey flannel squares. The searchlights lent a rhythmic illumination to the crowded, predawn barrack: ill-shod women making their skimpy toilet. "Listen to this, Jutka," Trudi dangled her cloth-wrapped feet. "It'll only take a minute."

"Go on! I'm listening."

"I was dreaming of this huge, round table surrounded by a dozen children—my own brood, not some kindergarten class. A checkered tablecloth was loaded with food: bread, milk, fruit, and a huge round of cheese. In the middle of it, an immense tureen of steaming *gulyás*. I grabbed a ladle, and filled my kids' bowls to the brim. The joy of it!"

"I hope it'll come true for you, Trudi," I chuckled.

She pursed her full lips: "A dozen kids . . . How about that? But it'll be tough to catch a husband. You know, Jutka, God is unfair to some of us women: only little kids think me pretty—that's why I became a kindergarten teacher."

I smiled at her, aping the gypsy soothsayer: "I see a handsome, robust mate in your future, my lady." Assuming my normal voice, I added half in jest: "Who cares about men? Tell me, Trudi, how was the *gulyás?*"

She slapped her bony thighs: "Stupid me, I never tasted it!"

Winter was spent battling for food. Luckily, we were three—loners often became lethargic. Magda was advantaged as a camp worker, and she managed to pilfer a carrot, a turnip, or some cabbage leaves almost every day—always sharing it with mother and me. Once she even brought us a few scraps of stewed beef. "It's SS food!" she panted, proudly. "I risked my life for it."

After we licked the last crumb, I thanked her profusely: "Best food I've tasted since we left home. Where did you get it, Magda?"

"Promise you won't throw up," she squeezed my hand. "I stole it from the Kommandant's dozing bloodhound."

Gnawing hunger often chased me to the garbage heap. One day, I was standing behind the factory kitchen, grinning contentedly at a three-quarters-rotted carrot I had just found, when I noticed a German woman staring at me. "She'll report it!" I trembled, but her eyes telegraphed only horror and pity. I've turned into a scavenger, I shuddered, and dropped my rotten carrot with disgust. I stopped digging for days.

By March, hunger became painful and scary. Walking down the forest path after night shift, I complained to mother: "I want to howl from hunger like a wolf." In desperation, she pilfered a big handful of vegetables the very next day. But she had been too greedy: her hoard of golden carrots dribbled from her dress like stolen nuggets.

"The Kommandant'll have your hair or worse!" Manci threatened.

"I did it for my child!" mother cried, and Manci did not report the incident.

One day, as Mother was racing along with half a stolen cabbage in each hand, she spied the Kommandant turning the corner. Instantly, mother slipped the two firm rounds under her blouse, proudly parading her newly jutting breasts: "Guten Tag, Kommandant!"

My riskiest enterprise was a joint venture with thirtyish Liz Ziegler, who had the reputation of having been rich and proud. Liz offered me a partnership to steal potatoes at night: she stood guard while I fished them out of an outdoor barrel. Since we had no means of cooking them, we lugged them to the factory hidden under our blouses, then we bartered them in sign language with some Lithuanian women. I dare say none of them guessed that one of their tattered customers had lived in a mansion only last spring.

Unfortunately, our precious barrel was dragged indoors a couple of days later, and our venture folded for lack of raw materials.

• • •

Late in winter, some Frenchmen informed us that the Americans had occupied nearby Kassel, and from then on we expected them in Lichtenau any day. The munitions factory ran out of chemicals, and the SS dragged a group of us high up into a black forest to build a new channel for a stream. Our train stopped at Helsa, a fairy-tale village nestled in an iceberg's lap, near Lichtenau. The houses were half-timbered, with gingerbread designs painted over their fronts.

"How idyllic," Éva marveled, "like an illustration for *Hansel and Gretel*."

"It might be the setting for an opera," breathed Meda Dános.

"Pfui!" Marcsa spat. "Shame on you, both. It's stinking German."

Our rows of fives climbed up a winding mountain pass, and I gasped at a wider and wider expanse of translucent sky and snow-capped ridges. "The Gothic gods chose a splendid habitat," I muttered. "It's heaven—for Germans."

Panting from the climb, mother spoke with effort: "Next year we'll visit the Tatras with papa. That'll be heaven . . ."

By mid-morning we reached a sun-drenched plateau, blanketed with half-thawed pine needles and patches of snow. The SS distributed road-building implements with an important air, but the work was a sham to keep us occupied: the frozen ground did not yield to the pickax.

As the sun neared its summit, the SS women bid us collect dry branches to build a camp fire. Busily roasting their aromatic sausages, the guards paid only slight attention to us. We made our modest holiday: munching bread, warming our fingers by the flames, taking leaks in the nearby woods. Daringly, I stayed behind in a sunlit clearing, hoping the bloodhounds wouldn't sniff me out. The warmed, moist earth exhaled the pungent aroma of decay and rebirth. A small bird was chirping on a pine branch, reminding me of Lőrincz Szabó's lilting poem, "Nyitnikék," about a tiny bird's endurance and faith: "Akinek tele rosszabb mint az enyém / és aki mégis csupa remény—as winter grows meaner and leaner / its song of hope thrills clearer and keener."

"We'll make it until spring," I told my feathered comrade.

Suddenly, Hyena, our homeliest overseer, startled me with her rough voice: "You're playing hooky, bitch!" she barked at me. "Instead of pissing, you're loafing here. Thinking of men, no doubt. Haha!" Mutely, I shook my head and started toward my comrades.

Hyena grabbed my arm and slapped me on the cheeks: "Don't lie to me!" she roared. "I can read your face. But dreaming is all that's left for you, bitch. After the war, you'll be transported to a desert island. No males—not even natives. Much use'll be your fancy looks, with snakes for company. Do you suppose the Americans will win the war? That would be your death sentence. We'll shoot you Jewish bitches before the Americans come—it's the Führer's decree. Your fate is sealed either way: No men. No sex. No seed of Sarah."

Hyena's threats brought sex fantasies: summer nights at Lake Balaton; love-making in a small boat that never tipped. The hero of my dreams was a stunning forced laborer whom I knew only by sight. I had named him "Discus Thrower" for his athletic build, Grecian profile, and the graceful way he hurled shells.

Other forces were also at work: war's end and spring's beginning. Éva Jámbor, my spectacled friend, had a proposal from a Dutch forced laborer. "He's handsome, he's blond," Éva blushed as she told me about him. "I don't know him, and he doesn't know me. Yet he wants to marry me after the war. Crazy, isn't it?"

"Not as crazy as you think."

Vera's Belgian admirer had more immediate plans. He told Vera that the SS were planning to transport all Jews before the Americans liberated Lichtenau. The Belgian promised to disconnect the electric wire fence and to liberate Vera as soon as the camp emptied. "I'll hide in camp while the rest of you leave," Vera confided in me.

"But where can you hide?" I asked, incredulous.

"I'll jump down a latrine hole. Pray for me, Jutka."

"You'd never be able to crawl out of there by yourself," I shivered. "Can you trust him?"

"Don't worry, Jutka," she tossed her bronze head, "I know my man."

I wished I could say the same for myself. My Frenchman and I had been flirting for several months, but only at a distance. He finally made contact a couple of days later. As our shift was trudging to work below his embankment, he stopped loading his shells to float a tiny paper airplane in my direction. Our big-nosed SS guard, Hyena, was constantly snooping at us in her pocket mirror, but this time she took no notice. One wing was addressed in French: TO BLUE KERCHIEF. Furtively, my comrades passed it along until it reached me. Quickly, I unfolded the paper plane and read the message: "I HAVE AN ESCAPE PLAN." For a moment, I thought of mother and Magda, but decided I would bring them along—hoping that my Frenchman had better plans than hiding in latrine holes.

A couple of days later, he launched another folded note in my direction. My face heating, I watched it float on a soft current—a paper carrier pigeon. Will it find me? It did, but I never got a chance to decipher the miniature lettering. Hyena swooped down while I was still unfolding the wings.

"I've got eyes in the back of my head!" the SS woman waved her pocket mirror victoriously. "The Kommandant'll shoot you for this, bitch." But next day, the Americans reached the outskirts of Lichtenau, and I escaped it.

During morning head count, the Kommandant announced above the rat-tat-tat of a nearby shell fire: "No one goes to the factory today. You'll plant gardens." The guards quickly distributed shovels and pickaxes and, ignoring the accelerating gunfire, made us dig garden plots. But within the hour they bid us return our tools to the storehouse.

Next, they handed out cotton prisoners' garb. Our soiled clothes were in shreds, and we pushed and screamed to get at the new striped dresses before the supply should run out. The noise was deafening. Neuman, the oldest of our three SS *Oberscharführers*, whom Magda used to call "Stepfather" because he used to give her extra food from time to time, turned purple. "Shut up!" he bellowed, and fired into the mob. A bullet hit Magda Braun of Kaposvár in the stomach. In the silence that ensued, she was dragged, bleeding, to the infirmary, while a swearing "Stepfather" trudged toward the Kommandant's barrack. The tumult continued, I got my dress, mother and Magda lost out.

Soon, the kapo whistled for another head count, our last *Zähl Appell* at Lichtenau. We were three short, which infuriated the SS, but there was no time for a recount; they hustled us to the railroad station to the accompaniment of accelerating gunfire.

Stretching my neck, we inspected the crowd: Vera seemed to be missing. Was it pity I felt, or envy? I thought of my Frenchman's aborted plans, and of handsome Vera neck-deep in excrement, and I wished I could pray for us both—to a god who would listen.

We rode a cattle train once more. Magda slipped away from her kitchen crew and joined our barrackmates. At night, we slept, tightly packed; during the day we sat cross-legged on the hay-strewn floor. Next morning, the engine stopped at a busy railroad station. Meda Dános knelt up to the window, and called out for everyone to hear: "It's Weimar!"

"Goethe's Weimar!" Liz echoed her ecstatically.

"Idiots," Marcsa spat with a grimace. She pushed through the squatting mob and lifting her ragged skirt, perched on the pail. "Germans are pigs, past or present," she pronounced, peeing noisily.

Soft-haired Edit, the former gimnazium teacher, waited for Marcsa to climb off the pail, then said in her calm, prim voice: "Weimar is a very special place. Does anyone want to hear the names of famous people connected with it?"

"Please, tell us, Professor," Éva said, making it sound like school.

Edit rose to her knees—the wagon being too low for standing—and clasping her emaciated hands as if in prayer, she intoned each name devoutly: "Johann Wolfgang Goethe, Friedrich Schiller, Franz Liszt, Walter Gropius."

Later, the engine pulled us onto a lone track and abandoned us there. I thought of Goethe's *Wanderers Nachtlied,* the poem I had found open at my grandfather Klein's death, and repeated it softly to myself: ". . . Warte nur balde, ruhest du auch—Wait, soon, you too shall rest . . ." I mustn't lose heart, I told myself.

From the north, we heard the constant rattle of bombs and guns: the Americans were near. "What's north of us, Professor?" Meda wanted to know.

Edit shook her head: "I studied here at Weimar for a year, but I never visited the villages." None of us had heard of the Buchenwald concentration camp, only a few kilometers away.

Those who had bread ate it in secret. Magda had stolen nine boiled potatoes from the SS just before we left—the greatest fortune we ever had. Guiltily, we munched one cold potato per person per night. They lasted us three days.

The bolted wagon held us for a week. The pessimists predicted our stay would end in death, but we told them to keep it to themselves. A group of us huddled together in a corner, some in rags, some in prisoners' garb, trying to amuse ourselves.

Mostly we sang or exchanged recipes. I recall a lengthy discussion about *rétes,* the incredibly flaky Hungarian strudel. Marcsa liked it filled with peppered fried cabbage, but the rest of us preferred it sweet, with apples, sour cherries, or creamed cottage cheese. Mrs. Weiss offered a novel version: "My cook used to bake it in flat layers," she said, smacking her lips, "then she would fill the cooled pastry with chocolate mousse and top it with swirls and swirls of whipped cream. Delicious!" While she pulled out her last half-slice of bread and munched it with a faraway look in her eyes, the women, most of whom used to bake their own desserts, offered dozens of ultra-rich recipes: mousses, *palacsintas, tortas*—everything topped with whipped cream or chocolate.

We did not always chat with folded hands; tall Puci Dukesz, our former barrack head, had a needle and lent it freely. I ripped a band from the hem of my striped dress, and sewed on a large pocket—to steal more efficiently wherever we landed next.

12
LIBERATION IN LEIPZIG
Leipzig, Germany • Spring 1945

OUR train had left Weimar just before the Americans arrived, and I did not expect to be freed at our next stop either—much less to meet my future husband there.

As we started our five-by-five march from the Leipzig railroad station, accompanied by our Lichtenau guards and dogs, I overheard the SS laughing and cheering: "Have you heard the latest? Our luck is changing!"

My pulse skipped a beat: what was happening?

The Kommandant and the Oberscharführer Zorbach—who had once surprised me as I washed myself naked in our Lichtenau barrack—walked by me. Zorbach sounded jubilant: "Roosevelt is dead; our Führer will win!"

"Oh, no!" I cried out in Hungarian.

"Shut up, you scum!" His stiff boot kicked me in the crotch. The excruciating pain in my most private flesh unnerved me completely. "All is lost, the Germans will win," I thought, desperately.

Éva Jámbor bent down to whisper: "Jutka, listen. Do you know who will be the next president? I've heard about him from my Dutch friend. Vice-President Truman—true man. Get it? He'll win the war, you'll see."

I got up, despite the pain, and let mother and Magda drag me along before the Oberscharführer could kick me again.

Herded by guards and hounds, we crossed a large section of Leipzig. As the pain subsided, I gazed around me: the afternoon sun flashed through a vast array of windowless arches, obscenely displaying their gutted insides. This was not the Leipzig I had read about, a city famed for its fairs, where Bach played the organ in Saint Thomas's Church. All around me, the ruins of ancient Rome seemed multiplied a thousand times.

"The Germans can't last," a comrade muttered. "They must be living like rats in the cellars."

I imagined a woman crawling on her knees, cradling an infant in front of her. "Serves them right!" I echoed—my voice a spiteful stranger's. What have I become?—I shuddered, shocked at my own words. Have I no pity left, not even for the children?

Just before nightfall, we arrived at Lager Tekla, a small Hungarian Jewish women's camp that had been half bombed out by the Americans. We were assigned two to a cot. Magda became separated from us because she still counted as a Lager worker and was given a cot in Manci's barrack. But at the first shriek of the sirens, she sneaked out to crawl in with us. The move probably saved her life: Manci's barrack was among those bombed out.

The kapo escaped with only a burned hand, but her friend, Klára, who had been given my job as cleaning woman to the Kommandant's mistress, was among the dead. By the light of the flames, I gazed at her scorched corpse in dread: Klára had taken my place.

At sunrise, we were herded to Schönau Lager on the outskirts of Leipzig, an immense prisoner-of-war camp with a wide view over the city. Next to us were barracks for captured French, Czech and Dutch soldiers, who wore their shabby uniforms without insignia. Despite the ban against fraternizing, the men flocked to our electric barbed wire fence, offering us bits of information. Several warned me of constant saturation bombing by Americans.

Sure enough, the sirens shrieked just before sunset. As the SS ran for shelter, I eyed the electric wire fence; there was no way to escape—not even in the event of a direct hit.

The man-made cataclysm approached with a relentless rhythm, never skipping a beat. Planes roared, bombs fell, fires exploded, always nearer and nearer. I watched, mesmerized, waiting to be engulfed by the approaching flames.

"Come, Jutka, everyone is going in," mother broke the spell. In the barrack, we lay down on the ground, waiting to perish by American bombardment.

The planes roared ever more threateningly, until they thundered just overhead. I expected to die the very next moment, but I felt detached and calm, less nervous than during a final exam.

The pilots continued on their dreadful way without discharging a single bomb over us, and we sprang to our feet, too stunned to celebrate. "What if they return with a fresh supply of bombs?" shuddered the pessimists, but the bombers skipped us routinely.

Three days later, as gunfire boomed in the west, the Kommandant called us for *Zähl Appell*. "We're moving east again," he barked, hoarsely, "this time on foot. Be prepared to run at a fast pace," he cautioned, "stragglers will be shot without mercy." Before dismissing us, the Kommandant solemnly added: "The disabled may remain in the infirmary. But I wouldn't stay if I were you."

Perplexed, a group of us confronted the kapo: "What to do with the sick, Manci?"

"Don't let them stay in the infirmary if they can walk at all!" she cautioned, the twitch of her eye betraying her anxiety.

Worried about mother, I asked advice of a Frenchman across the fence. "The SS brought in a truckful of kerosene," he told me in a whisper. "They'll be setting the camp on fire, we figure."

I ran for Magda, and we discussed it in a hurry.

"Rózsi cannot survive a forced march," she warned. "Would you leave her dying by the wayside?"

"Of course not."

"You see, it's dangerous to stay, but suicide to go," Magda shuddered, and we agreed to stay.

Mother welcomed our decision with her usual optimism: "We'll be liberated within the week."

As we entered the spacious infirmary, we found only six occupants in it, all desperately ill—including Magda Braun, who had been shot in the stomach. The rest of our comrades had all chosen to march, despite their sorry state. I felt myself go rigid. Could we three be right, and all those hundreds be wrong? But there was no time to hesitate: our Italian doctor, Luciana Nissim, told mother to crawl into bed at once and she let Magda and me sneak under her blanket. Quickly, mother pulled the covers over our heads. "You're so thin, you're hardly noticible," Luciana assured us before she left.

Within minutes, the door opened, and I recognized Hyena's rasping laughter. "No malingerers today!" the SS guard jeered. "Don't you worry," she reassured mother in a falsely honeyed tone. "We'll get you by truck. You'll see your daughters tomorrow."

"I know I will," mother nudged us gently with her toes.

Early next morning, I awoke to two SS women appearing at the door. "Mach schnell!—Hurry up!" they called, and the nine of us escaped Lager Schönau before its destruction.

The SS led us through the gate, and guided us into a wide open field. Magda and I carried Magda Braun sitting on our interlaced hands, her spindly arms around our shoulders.

"Let's gang up on the SS and grab their pistols," I told Magda, as I surveyed the vast field surrounded by gaping ruins. "There isn't another German in sight."

"Forget it," Magda shook her head. "We don't even know how to pull the trigger."

The SS women herded us to a large garrison, situated by a single pair of railroad tracks. One of them pointed at a row of idling coaches stretching beyond the curve: "This afternoon, you'll be going east by passenger train! We trust that you'll repay us for saving your lives, when the time comes. Auf Wiedersehen."

We entered a large hall swarming with women. They were not concentration camp prisoners but forced laborers, a distinction immediately evident from their fleshier look and their colorful peasant outfits with wide skirts and flowered kerchiefs. I wished I could understand their Slavic chatter.

Suddenly, I noticed three stately, well-dressed blondes in animated conversation with an SS officer. As soon as the SS departed, I edged close to them. The women switched from German to Polish, then to French, so I could understand every word they said: the SS had allowed them to stay behind to be liberated.

"Pardonnez moi," I interrupted them, "I overheard your plans. I'd like to stay with you, together with my comrades. We're only nine."

They were aghast, but it did not take me long to strike a bargain: I promised to keep their secret, and they agreed to hide us. The kapo noticed our blue-and-white triangular emblem. "The SS may return for you Jews," she warned, as she led us to a windowless cubbyhole in the basement. "If they do, I'll tell them that this is a quarantine for contagious diseases. Take off your clothes and hide them well, then wrap yourselves into these blankets. Oh, yes, be sure not to come anywhere near us. Do you hear!"

"Jawohl, Kapo," I nodded, feeling more of an outcast than before. When I heard the passenger train leaving, I was once more overcome by doubt. Had we made a fatal decision?

Late that night, some Polish women dragged three men shrieking in pain thumping down the stairs. I felt nauseated: the men were burned to charcoal, their skin and clothes hardly distinguishable. The women deposited them into the nook next to ours. The former kapo told us that they were Czech prisoners of war who had barely escaped from a neighboring Lager—probably our former camp, Schönau, we figured.

• • •

My worst fears were confirmed just before dawn, as I awoke to a blinding light. The Polish kapo held a flashlight, as an SS officer pointed his pistol. "Are these wretches Jewish?" he thundered.

"They're Polish," the kapo lied. "Watch out, they're highly contagious."

"Let them kiss my boot then," snarled the SS. "Say something in Polish, bitch!" he roared, kicking us each in turn. "Talk, or I'll shoot you in the head."

"They're too sick to talk," said the kapo, but the officer continued to test us, his heavy boot rolling us around like sacks.

I closed my eyes, holding my blanket tightly around me. What if a feverish comrade cries out in Hungarian?

"Let the swine rot in their own filth," roared the SS at last, and off he went, cursing.

The kapo returned, radiant: "Thank God, we're free of him!"

• • •

We spent the next two-and-a-half days neither as prisoners nor free. The Germans had fled, but the Americans hadn't come yet. The kapo let us go upstairs, where we found some fancy conserves in a small cupboard formerly reserved for the SS: roast pork, goose liver paté, and sardines. We thought it may be our last chance to eat well, so we gorged ourselves on the rich fare. No wonder we spent the whole night expelling it from both ends.

Freedom came on the third day, not in the shape of a victorious army—with drums and generals as we had dreamt—but in the person of a dusty American telephone operator. We rushed out as he appeared on the road, a tiny uniformed form on a motorcycle. The Polish girls pulled him off the seat and hugged him from all sides, but we stood by, trying to take it in.

"You girls just wait," he protested with a flushed face. "Thousands more will pour in tomorrow. Please excuse me; I must fix some telephone wires." The next moment, he vanished like an apparition we had dreamt.

The following day, April 20, 1945, we were officially freed, but were still too dazed to fully appreciate it. The Americans moved us into a second-rate hotel in one of Leipzig's half-bombed-out districts. The nine of us Hungarian Jews were given rooms along the same corridor, Mother, Magda, and I sharing a triple. After a nourishing meal, mother lay down, thankful for a real bed, and so did our sick comrades. Only Magda and I decided to go out. "For heaven's sake, don't get lost!" mother fretted as we embraced her.

The German soldiers had fled, the civilians hid. The main thoroughfares were completely taken over by motorized American troops, tossing cigarettes and Hershey bars at the throngs of liberated slaves who shouted and sang in a cacophony of tongues. All of Europe seemed represented.

"It's a veritable tower of Babel!" Magda shook her head. "I can hardly believe this."

The truth was, I could hardly believe it either. I wished we could be with our Lichtenau comrades, or in Kaposvár, with family and friends, instead of with this wildly celebrating mob whose speech often seemed foreign to me.

I answered Magda with something like: "Don't you just love it though?" and I spun her around, until she laughed, helplessly: "Enough, enough! You make me dizzy."

"Look," I flapped my arms, feeling more relaxed and happy, "I think I could swim up into the air! We're free! Really free!" Magda soon caught the fever, and we sang and danced, blending into the ecstatic mob.

Just before sunset, my intoxication gave way to more practical concerns: I joined a crowd that was looting a vacant factory, dragging a reluctant Magda with me. "Look at these clothes!" I marveled, digging out a freshly laundered salt-and-pepper coverall. "No more striped garb for me!"

"Let's go, Jutka," Magda pulled me away. "It's getting late. Your mother will be worried."

"I'll just grab some office supplies; I'll be back in a minute." My loot: a dozen pencils, but no paper.

Magda and I returned to our hotel, where we resided for three more weeks, together with the Polish women who had been liberated with us and with some French girls we had never met before. Our jubilation soon gave way to impatience: there was no transportation home, no mail or telephone to get news about family or friends. I sent messages to my American uncle, Dr. Francis Magyar, by dozens of American soldiers, but there was no way to receive an answer. Worst of all, our army rations were diminishing at an alarming rate. We suspected the former Polish kapo, our onetime benefactor, of being the chief culprit. An aristocrat who did not dare return to Poland, she probably bartered away our food for gold. Magda and I began to worry about all nine of us, especially mother, who was still weak and deathly pale from nine months of starvation.

13
My American Captain
Leipzig, Germany • May 15–July 3, 1945

"**H**OW did you two ever happen to meet?" people often ask us when we travel—referring to my Hungarian accent and my husband's New England twang.

Ike will look at me and laugh: "Well, it all started with a slice of salami . . ." And the tale then unfolds in its meandering way, told from our different perspectives.

• • •

May 15, 1945: that's the day it really started.

The morning began dismally. Magda called us to the window, pressing a thin slice of salami to the pane. "Jutka, Rózsi, come, see! This is all the meat we're getting today." Through the particles of gristle and meat, we viewed the bombed-out ruins across the street.

"Szivtelen lengyelek!—Heartless Poles!" mother sputtered. "They must be selling our rations on the black market."

"We'll be starving again," I shuddered. "It's getting worse every day."

"Let's complain to the Americans," Magda suggested, and we took off for the Military Goverment—with our three slices of salami in hand.

The MG headquarters was located in one of the few impressive buildings left in Leipzig. Hundreds of shabby petitioners like us queued up under its vaulted ceiling, inching along the vast corridors and up the ample staircase. Reluctantly, we joined them. It was about a month after liberation, and Magda and I had nearly regained our strength and former shapes—minus an inch or so around the waist—but mother

A Jewish service in Leipzig conducted by a U.S. army chaplain (May 1945). We three are on the right, our comrades are among the women on the left. The sickly gentleman in the front row was a seriously disabled veteran of World War I, and therefore exempt from deportation. (He and his wife were the only Jews allowed to remain in Leipzig through World War II.)

was still bony and weak. "You can't stand in line for hours, Rózsi," Magda fretted, but mother insisted on staying.

Uniformed Americans sailed by singly or in pairs, looking fit and carefree. Despite my baggy coveralls and wooden shoes, I thought myself quite attractive, but here, on their own turf, the troops ignored us. Magda and I enjoyed ourselves just the same, scrutinizing the men, especially the blacks, whom we found exotic. We had never seen a black person before, and the Hungarian translation of negroid, *szerecsen* (which I liked better than *néger*), had a fascinating ring to it.

Suddenly, an elegant officer stepped in front of me, clicking the fanciest pair of boots I had ever seen: "Guten Tag, Fraülein." I sized him up quickly: early forties, beige gabardine uniform immaculately pressed. To my unsophisticated eyes, he looked fancy enough for a general. I caught the name Switgall as he introduced himself, but not his rank.

"May I inquire what nationality you ladies might be?" he asked, politely, in German.

"Ungarische Judinnen—Hungarian Jewish women," I told him, so as not to be taken for Nazis.

"Magyar is the only European language I don't speak," he smiled, apologetically.

A boyish, wiry soldier then joined us, wearing combat breeches and dusty boots. "Captain Bergman," he introduced himself in German, bowing politely. To my mind, he seemed too young to be a captain.

"My comrade tells me that you resemble a charming cousin of his," the "General" winked at me as if to say: "A likely story." At this, I doubted the young man's rank as much as my supposed resemblance to his cousin—but it never occurred to me to doubt his name, Bergman.

"You really do look like my cousin," the captain earnestly protested. He had a candid, winning smile, and I decided to believe him. "I just wondered whether we might be related." We compared ancestors, but without success, and they soon left us with the customary "Auf Wiedersehen—see you again."

It was mid-afternoon when mother, Magda, and I finally reached the head of the line. "What do you want?" an American officer yawned at us from behind his massive desk.

"A transport to Hungary!" mother blurted.

His face was blank. "If it were up to me, I'd like to pack you off this very minute."

Magda produced the salami, and started to spill our grievances, but the officer dismissed her in mid-sentence: "Your female squabbles are none of my business. Those Polish ladies may not find you people so congenial to live with."

"An antisemite if I ever saw one," mother declared as we left.

"An American antisemite?" I shuddered. "That just can't be, Mama."

"I wish we had asked those nice officers to help us," Magda commented.

I had a sharp twinge of regret. Why hadn't I acted a little more pleasant to them? I could see very well that Captain Bergman had been interested in me, and I certainly liked his looks. Now, we'll never see them again.

The Polish women continued to cheat us of our rations, but we supplemented them with bread obtained on the black market. The American servicemen soon learned to recognize our concentration camp emblems, and they often tossed us chocolate bars and cigarettes on the street. One even handed me a slightly used white blouse with a brightly striped skirt, and another gave me a woman's bicycle, a real treasure in those days.

"No, thank you, it's too much," I refused him at first.

"Don't worry," the soldier protested in German. "I don't want anything in return." To prove it, he showed me his army orders, which called for him to report to headquarters at once. "We'll be fighting again by tomorrow," he murmured.

"Oh, no!" I cried, imagining him bleeding from a gunshot wound. "Is the war still going on?"

"For me it is," he sighed. "Take this lousy bicycle, kid, or I'll give it to a German girl."

"Don't do that," I grabbed the handlebars. "Thank you, and best of luck."

Next day, May 21, I was happily circling among the ruins when I noticed the sign "To Markleeberg." I had heard about a group of Hungarian Jewish women living there. I now pedaled off in a hurry—as if keeping an appointment.

I was amazed to find the rich suburb untouched by bombs, and a group of Hungarian Jewish women occupying a former SS camp in the middle of a lavish neighborhood. I saw no one from Kaposvár, but the women treated me like a friend, inviting me for dinner—outdoors, at picnic tables. I marveled at the nourishing meal: creamed spinach, cheese omelette, rye bread, and fresh rhubarb compote—most of the ingredients bartered from a nearby farmer for PX coffee and cigarettes. Quickly, I arranged for us to move in with them.

Early next morning, the nine of us left Leipzig for Markleeberg, about five kilometers away. Magda Braun, who was slowly recovering from the gunshot wound, was riding the bar of my bicycle as I pushed it along. Luckily, we had no luggage. After a delicious dinner and a nap, we transformed our drab room: two mattresses made a corner couch, a pile of SS blankets served for bedspreads and rugs. Mother placed a brilliant arrangement of wild flowers on the windowsill.

"The place is fit for company," I joked—certainly never expecting to entertain any. But as we stepped out to inspect our fancy neighborhood, we nearly collided with a jeep, and in it I recognized the same two officers we had met at MG headquarters. This time both men looked very smart, and I was glad I was wearing my freshly washed white blouse with my multi-striped skirt.

Switgall, who was driving, slammed on the brakes, his black button eyes dancing in the tanned, round face. "Didn't we meet you lovely ladies in Leipzig?"

Captain Bergman jumped out and grabbed an oily funnel from the back that held three spotless oranges. "Do you care to have some fruit?" he offered it to mother as if he were handling a silver dish.

"Do oranges still exist?" I laughed when he brought it to me. I was completely charmed by him.

We shook hands, Captain Bergman holding mine, it seemed, a little longer than was necessary. "You live in Markleeberg?" he gave me an astonished glance.

"We just moved here," I grinned.

"That's amazing! Listen, Fred," he turned to the general, "do you believe in Fate?" It appeared that they had just come to Markleeberg looking for a camera.

The "general" jokingly asked mother whether we had any room to spare, but she shook her head: "Sorry, we still live in a barrack."

"Why not in a fine home like that?" Switgall pointed at the opulent establishment on the corner. "Haven't the Germans taken away yours?"

Mother couldn't have agreed with him more, and she promptly invited them to see our spartan accommodations. Magda led the way, Switgall drove mother slowly in the jeep, and the handsome young captain walked with me. Our comrades gaped at the procession we made.

Switgall complimented us on our cozy room, confessing that our lodgings were outside their jurisdiction.

"That's all right, officer," mother sighed.

"Please call me Fred," he urged her, "and my comrade, Ike—like General Eisenhower."

"No resemblance," Ike protested.

After the first meeting, they visited us daily. It appeared that they were both Jewish and obviously educated, but there was a world of difference in their styles: Fred was an ebullient Polish refugee with a penchant for classy living, and Ike a low-key, third-generation New Englander. Fred often got into lively discussions with mother and Magda, gesticulating freely, while Ike and I sat silently on the corner sofa, our hands instinctively reaching for each other.

From the start, mother treated them both like family, and when Ike first offered to take me for a ride in the jeep, she did not object. From then on, Ike and I took long drives daily, chatting in French. My English was not fluent enough, and French seemed more intimate to us than German.

Before long, Ike told me that he worked in Army Intelligence. "The name Bergman is just for the Germans," he said, "I'm really Irving Isaacson, in peacetime a lawyer in Maine." He disclosed that Fred was not an officer at all, but only a sergeant, assigned to him as his interpreter.

"But why the fancy uniform?" I asked, and Ike explained that it was permitted in the OSS, the Office of Strategic Services, the outfit they worked for. "Mostly, I keep mine in my rucksack," he grinned.

As Ike came to know me better and to trust me, he felt free to tell me about his army experiences. It was an entire world away from my own, and I couldn't get enough of it.

"How did you ever happen to get into the OSS?" I wanted to know.

"Just by the grace of God," he laughed. "Mostly, I guess, because I had smiled nicely at some British colonel, and nothing more." That didn't sound quite right to me, and I pressed him for more. "Well, if you really want to know, the whole thing was a total mistake by the army. It happened like this. Toward the end of last July, I was in a replacement camp in England, waiting to go to Normandy. Well, one day I got orders to report to the OSS in London. I didn't know what the OSS was all about, and neither did anybody else. Anyway, I reported to their office in London, and nobody could figure out what I was doing there. They told me to go away for a week and to come back. It was something unheard of.

"When the week was up, I did come back, and they suggested that I talk with some of their officers to see if anybody had a place for me. I didn't want to go back to the infantry but all I had to offer them didn't seem very useful; a Harvard Law School degree, four years of infantry training in radio and telephone communications, a drop of French, a dash of German—and me.

"It just so happens that one of the officers they sent me to was a big, fat British colonel, with a total upperclass accent and everything that goes with it. He was just a perfect specimen. He listened carefully to me, and seemed to show some interest. After a few hems and haws, he came out in his total British accent: 'That's all very interesting, and we might possibly have a place for you here. However, do you mind jumping?'

"Well, what was I going to say? So, I asked: 'What do you mean by jumping?'

"'Why, parachute jumping, of course,' he said. Now I had a real problem, don't you agree? Do I leave this outfit and get shipped to Normandy, or do I get involved with some unkown business, involving parachuting? It took only seconds to decide. 'It sounds just great. Count me in.' So, you see, that's me and the OSS. Wasn't that ridiculous?"

I told Ike about my own split-second decisions during crises, and he listened, understanding me completely, it seemed.

But mostly we spoke about books, sailing, and sports. "Do you play tennis?" I asked him once, imagining us tossing a white ball across a pink court.

"I do, but I prefer squash, though to tell you the truth, I haven't played either in years. Not since I joined the army, in January of '41."

"But that's four and a half years ago! That's even before America entered the war."

"Actually, I volunteered."

"Out of patriotism? Or because you are Jewish?"

"Well, neither, really. To tell you the truth, I had just recently gotten out of law school and I was a little bored with my father's law practice. Besides, I had just broken up with my girlfriend."

"I see," I nodded, appreciating his honesty. "How old were you then?"

"Twenty-four."

"But you don't look a day older than that now."

"I know," he laughed. "I used to regret looking that young. But not anymore."

"Tell me about parachute jumping. It sounds scary."

He went on to tell me about jump training and the various characters involved. "Really, it was quite a lot of fun," he asserted. "You know, it's one of the most beautiful feelings in the world to look up and see that huge parachute open up above you, all nice and full."

"It sounds more exciting than the war novels I've read," I said, enchanted, and we were off, talking about books. I found him better read than most of my Hungarian acquaintances—but very nonchalant about it. I loved that about him.

One sunny day, as we skipped out for a ride, we found a cherubic little German boy sitting in his puddle on the driver's seat. I expected Ike to get really upset, but he just lifted off the toddler gently—avoiding his dripping little breeches. "Wass haben *Sie* hier gemacht—What have you done here?"—he softly rebuked the child for the mess, and placed him carefully on the ground. I burst out laughing. "What's so funny?" he turned to me.

"You called him *Sie,* Ike," I explained, "it's like saying 'Sir' to an infant." But I really laughed to see a soldier so gentle with a baby.

Near the end of May, Ike informed me that he and Fred would be taking a trip to Eastern Europe.

"Will you be gone for long?"

"It's hard to tell."

"Will it be dangerous?"

"I don't think so, but that's what we'll want to find out for sure. If we are successful, we'll be the first Allied personnel to report on the conditions in the Russian zone."

"Where do you plan to go?"

"Well, first we'll take a trial run into Czechoslovakia, and if that goes well, then on to Poland, or maybe even to Hungary. Would you like to show me around in Kaposvár?"

"You'd better hurry," I replied wistfully, thinking of Peti. "You never know, I may be a married woman by then." Ike thought that I was just teasing, because I had never mentioned my boyfriend to him.

• • •

Ike and Fred left for Czechoslovakia on May 29, having hidden some of their documents under our beds. "Be sure to burn them if we don't come back," Ike warned us.

I fretted about him during the day, I dreamt about him during the night, and I was overjoyed to welcome him back a couple of days later.

"How did it go? Was it risky?" I probed.

"Not really." I did not believe him, and I hated to see him leave for Poland the very next day.

During their absence, an American officer came to our camp. He assembled us rather formally, and announced that Leipzig and vicinity would be taken over shortly by the Russians. He promised us direct transportation to Budapest within the week.

At this, my comrades rejoiced with loud cries and cheers, but my throat constricted in anguish. What if we should leave before Ike gets back from Poland? Would I ever see him again? Now that my life could be carefree and happy, why had it become so complex?

The passenger train for Hungary pulled into Markleeberg some two weeks after the men had left for Poland. Magda was for burning Ike's papers, but I protested: "You can't do that! Not yet! Not yet!"

"What's the matter with you, Jutka?" mother felt my forehead. "You're hot. You feel feverish to me."

The fever mounted all day, and at night I dreamt of Ike, sensuous dreams such as I had never had before. I woke before dawn, hot and trembling. Now I really wanted to stay behind, but how could I manage it? Should mother and Magda give up their chance to go home just because of me? And what about Peti? For the first time in months, I could picture him clearly, blond hair, blue eyes, smiling at me beckoningly. Was he already at home, waiting for me? I loved him, I told myself, but differently. How to resolve the conflict?

Anguish fed the fever, and fever fed the anguish; by morning, I was delirious. Mother rushed out and soon brought back a German woman physician who examined me closely. "Your daughter mustn't leave on the transport," I heard her in a daze. "This might turn into pneumonia; a trip like that could be fatal."

"We'll stay?" I whispered, hardly believing.

"We'll stay, sweetheart," mother hugged me. "Of course, we'll stay."

I was delirious again when the transport pulled out the next day. Mother later related to me how she ran out on the street, pacing frantically about. What to do? The rumors she had heard were terrifying, and she knew that three lone women mustn't face the drunken troops in a deserted camp. But where could we go? Whom could we turn to for help?

A refined German housewife suddenly appeared around the corner, with a small wicker basket on her arm—identical to mother's in Kaposvár. Mother ran up to her, introduced herself, and quickly explained our predicament. The lady offered us refuge.

Two days later, I woke from delirium in a shiny brass bed, between white linen sheets such as I had not seen since I left home. Was I dreaming? A soldier was standing by my bed, holding my hand. I pulled myself up on my elbows, to see better.

Ike bent down, and gently kissed me on the forehead: "How do you feel? Any better?"

"Ike, you've come back," I whispered.

Toward the end of June, mother, Magda, and I left Leipzig, about ten days before it was taken over by the Russian army. Ike drove us to Berneck-am-Fichtelgebirge, a picturesque resort town in Bavaria. Fred was waiting for us in a charming house he had requisitioned from a former Nazi official. There, I recovered quickly.

In the garden at Berneck-am-Fichtelgebirge (July 1945). I wear the bathing suit mother fashioned for me from some rag.

Ike typed away steadily on his OSS report on Poland, but he spent his afternoons with me. Mother fashioned for me a black-and-white bathing suit from a T-shirt she had found in a drawer, and Ike pulled out some bathing trunks he hadn't used in years. We found a tin tub and an outdoor shower, and we frolicked in our lovely garden that rose to the hills behind the house.

"Aki él az mind, mind örüljön—All who live, rejoice, rejoice," I translated my Auschwitz motto for him into French. Just an afternoon like this with Ike was worth surviving for, I felt.

At the end of June, Fred picked up a rumor that a transport would soon be leaving for Budapest. Mother and Magda started preparing for the journey, anxious to return, but again I was frantic. If only I could stay a while longer. Ike and I had met only six weeks ago, and we had spent such a small portion of it together.

● ● ●

Next day, I woke to a sunny July third, a ripe summer morning—my twentieth birthday. I leaned out a casement window to sniff moist earth, raspberries, and roses. "All who live, rejoice, rejoice," I repeated to myself, expectantly.

Fred had bartered some PX coffee and cigarettes for farm-fresh food: a freshly plucked chicken, a basketful of sweet peas, a dozen eggs, and a pound of sweet-churned butter. Mother prepared a torte I often dreamt about in Lichtenau: seven layers of delicate chocolate frostings and a caramel glaze as glossy as glass—affectionately called *dobos torta* by Hungarians—after the chef's name who had invented it. (*Dobos* means drummer, and the torte resembles a drum.)

The presents were handmade by mother and Magda, or bartered for by Fred and Ike. Ike brought in his gifts one by one, each accompanied by a witty note in French, English, or German. I was enchanted.

During dinner Fred sparkled with funny stories from many countries—and I laughed until my last birthday suddenly leapt to mind: Kaposvár's municipal stables; our honeymooners, Sári Holló and Laci Dénes; uncle Bandi Pogány emerging from the torture chambers. I remembered my friends wishing me a happy birthday, whispered by Peti's mother like a prayer: "Isten éltessen—God keep you, Jutka," she had whispered. "Take care of my son."

I glanced at Ike, and the visions vanished.

After the *dobos torta* and coffee, Ike and I climbed to the top of the terraced garden, past the roses and raspberry beds. I was mesmerized by starry skies and earthy smells. A full moon beamed improbably near, bewitchingly romantic. On the garden bench, Ike embraced me, and we kissed—for the first time.

Our engagement picture (July 4, 1945). Ike took this snapshot of us with his self-timer. I wear my only skirt—of many colors.

"Someday soon, I'll be going home to Maine," he told me hours later. "You'd love it there. Forests and beaches. A thousand lakes. A good place to raise children. Will you come with me?"

He was proposing marriage!

"You hardly know me!"—I blurted, though I barely knew him either. But I quickly gathered my wits just as I used to do in camp—the moment demanded it. Hurriedly, I weighed my options. Peti or Ike? Paris or the Maine woods? Books or babies? Poetry or sex?

Peti would never forgive me—I thought with a pang—but the decision was mine, to applaud or regret for life.

Averting my face, I glanced at the stars. Perched by the chimney, I recognized an old friend, Ursa Major, unchanged and intimate. He had tracked me from Kaposvár to Auschwitz, to Lichtenau, to Berneck. "Ike," I whispered, my voice barely audible, "can you see the Great Bear in Maine?"

"You bet your life you can!" he laughed, taking me in his arms again.

It was well past midnight—and our Bear winking from afar— when we came skipping down the terraced garden. On the moonlit path, our giant shadows trembled.

EPILOGUE
RETURN␣TO KAPOSVÁR
Kaposvár, Hungary • July 3–July 9, 1977

I SPENT my nineteenth birthday, July 3, 1944, in the stables of my
hometown, Kaposvár—before deportation to Auschwitz.

On my twentieth, I became engaged.

I observed my twenty-first at my in-laws' summer place in Popham Beach, Maine—a married woman, five months pregnant.

Thirty-three years later, our family celebrated my birthday—and
the Fourth of July—with a traditional Maine clambake in our garden—
with flowers, peas, and strawberries picked on the spot. There were
nine of us: mother, Ike, our three grown children with their spouses,
and myself.

After dinner, my husband recorded the year's events in a note-
book he kept in a humorous vein. "Jutka quit as Dean of Students
after eight years," Ike wrote about me. "Bates College will never be
the same."

"True," I chuckled, still amused by the fact that I, Jutka Magyar of
Kaposvár, should have been dean at this venerable New England
college.

Next day, July 5, 1977, my daughter, Ilona, and I departed for
Hungary—exactly thirty-three years from the day I left it by cattle car.

Our family calendar marked off a generation: Ilona, a brown-
eyed, brown-haired, fascinating young woman, was in her twenties,

but she looked about nineteen, as I was then. As we reclined in our seats, Ilona and I talked about our work—I was contemplating a return to teaching mathematics and computer science in the fall, and Ilona was an instructor of English literature at Smith College.

Over the Atlantic, Ilona shifted our conversation to the war. "Mom, you named John for your father, you named him for a Holocaust victim. Why not me?"

"But I did, Ilona," I smiled involuntarily. "I named you for my best friend, Ilona Pogány."

"You never told me."

"Of course I did. John mentioned it the other day. You just blocked it out."

Ilona's eyes deepened: "Do you know why? John and I had more than our share of nightmares as kids."

"And Mark?"

"He seems immune to it."

• • •

Ilona and I changed planes in Zurich, embarking for Budapest. As we lost altitude, I glimpsed through the porthole a familiar sight: a double row of poplars slicing the green terrain. In childhood they seemed to prove the theory of parallel lines to me—meeting at infinity. A sentimentally patriotic song welled up from my girlhood, spinning in my brain like a gramophone record: "Táltos paripámon haza szállok / Oda hív fű, fa, lomb, virág.—I fly home on my winged horse / beckoned by grass, trees, and flowers." I found myself weeping.

The attendant announced in both English and Hungarian: "Buckle your seat belts, ladies and gentlemen, we are about to descend to Budapest."

As the wheels crunched to the ground, Hungarian commands reached me from the outside, reminding me of the Nazi times. "I'm not getting out, Ilona," I groaned. "I want to fly back. My friends will show you around." But Ilona coaxed me off the plane, and by the time we reached the terminal I felt better. "I'm embarrassed," I apologized. "Momentary insanity."

At the baggage claim, a mustachioed, well-groomed young Hungarian stood next to Ilona. "Sir, how much should I tip the porter?" I asked him in hesitant Hungarian—I hadn't spoken it in decades, not even with my mother.

He explained, then added with a smile: "You have a trace of a foreign accent, Madam."

"That's what they tell me when I speak English," I laughed.

"Have you been abroad for a long time?"

"Thirty-three years."

"You must have left at the end of the war," he glanced at me, questioningly.

"I never *left*," I snapped, my throat constricting. "I was *taken*. To Auschwitz. By cattle car."

"He looks shocked," Ilona turned to me. "What did you tell him?"

I translated, adding with a shudder: "He must be a Nazi. It was the German sympathizers who left at the end of the war. I guess he took me for another."

"He is too young to be a Nazi," Ilona shook her head. "Born after the war, like me. Relax. You aren't yourself today."

But fury held me like a vise: "A Nazi's son then. What's the difference?"

Our luggage came, and Ilona was about to lift it when the young man sprang to help. Backed against the flow of traffic, he grabbed my hand and filled it with Hungarian coins. "For the porter," he told me, "it's just the right amount. "Csókolom—I kiss you." Stunned, I translated for Ilona.

"Why is he so intimate?" she frowned.

"Maybe he wants to make a profit," I speculated, not realizing that *csókolom* was the new, shortened form of *Kezét csókolom*—I kiss your hand, a greeting familiar to me in childhood. Offended, I handed him a ten-forint note.

"Oh, no," he pushed the bill back, and bending, he kissed my hand in the old-fashioned manner: "Isten hozta; haza hozta—God brought you; brought you home."

•　•　•

Some three-quarters of an hour later, Ilona and I arrived at the elegant Grand Hotel of Margit Island, situated on the lovely island park between Buda and Pest that I remembered so well from childhood. The taxi driver cheated us on the fare, but what did it matter?

My former boyfriend, a greying professor, was waiting for us with a bouquet of long-stemmed roses. "Dr. Péter Hanák," I introduced him to Ilona.

"Peti!" Ilona smiled, shaking hands. "It seems as if I have always known you."

Peti accompanied us to our airy room overlooking the island park, and I ran for the bottle of Cointreau we bought at the Amsterdam duty-free shop. "This calls for a celebration," I smiled, pouring the golden liqueur into clumsy water goblets.

"Such old-fashioned courtesies," teased the professor, raking his blond hair turned platinum. He clicked his glass to mine, and toasted me: "Happy Birthday! Éltessen! Do you know what it means, Ilona?"

"Vivat! " she cheered. "Lechayim! To life!"

"To our children!" I clicked my glass to Peti's.

"To our spouses!" he smiled, clearing my conscience at last. I must have made the right choice—for both of us—by marrying Ike.

• • •

On our first night, Ilona and I had dinner with my mother's cousin, Manci Fülöp, a pleasantly plump woman with charming dimples. She took us to a small Buda restaurant, with white tablecloths and Gypsy music. I played the American tourist quite successfully, until the *primás* started to play "A Vén Cigány—Ancient Gypsy," one of my father's favorite songs. My father had been buried at Mühldorf Lager in a mass grave, and I felt as if at long last I were attending his funeral. I hid my head in my arms to muffle the sobs.

After dinner, I wanted to go to bed, but Manci had invited some Kaposvár acquaintances to meet us at the hotel. The conversation centered on past family and friends, most of them dead.

Next day, Ilona and I left for our pilgrimage to Kaposvár.

• • •

The afternoon train ride was uneventful until a buxom housewife entered our second-class compartment. "I'm going home to Kaposvár," she mentioned in the accents of my hometown: "Are you getting out there?"

"Igen," I nodded, clenching my fists. "I was born and raised in Kaposvár."

"Really?" she marveled, eyeing my American shoes. "Visiting family?"

Mutely, I shook my head, then spit it out: "Most of my family was killed during the war."

"At Auschwitz?"

I nodded without a word.

"How dreadful!" she shuddered. "D'you know what's the worst mistake the Nazis made?"

"No," I sighed, stunned by her question.

"They should have gassed all the Gypsies instead!"

I refused her offer to drive us to our hotel.

Luggage in hand, Ilona and I walked from the familiar Kaposvár railroad station to the Hotel Dorottya—formerly Turul. "This is Count István Tisza Street 12, where my grandfather Klein used to live and where he died," I said, as we walked past the familiar two-story building.

"Let's rest tonight," Ilona suggested. "You must be exhausted."

At the hotel, I felt like making contact with someone, so I briefly telephoned a former classmate I vaguely remembered, the only one whose married name I obtained in Budapest. Afterward, Ilona and I had dinner and went to bed.

That night I had a recurring dream.

• • •

The dream starts with a sudden feeling of unease. My throat tightens, and I feel a childish sense of abandonment. I am a shy, sensitive toddler—as I was when Ilona Pogány and I first became playmates.

"Ilona doesn't come to play," I wail. "She doesn't love me anymore."

Then I become my present self, levelheaded and mature, and set out to find her. "Ilona," I want to tell her, "we must see each other more often."

I find myself in front of her house, at Castle Street, Kaposvár. A hazy figure stands about twenty paces away. Though blurred and two-dimensional, she is definitely Ilona: the slim, compact figure, the honey-colored face, the familiar arms. But she is a towhead again, and her soft hair bobbed with bangs. Why the childish hair with the grown-up face?

"I've missed you, Ilona," I want to say, "I've missed you for a long time." But I feel painfully shy, and I run toward her on infant legs, mutely waving my arms.

At this, she recedes beyond vacant Castle Street, above the Cser Forest, into a fading Kaposvár sky.

"Stay!" I beg with my whole being—I am the girl, the woman, and the child. "Stay, Ilona!"

• • •

I woke from this dream, missing my husband at my side. Ilona slept. "See you at breakfast," I left her a scrawled note.

The hotel clerk was shocked as he pointed at the clock: "It's four in the morning, Madam! And it's pouring out. At least take an umbrella along."

But I welcomed the rain; it diluted the tears as I walked the ill-lit streets of my hometown. A song came to me, a song we used to sing in Auschwitz: "Fölöttem sír az ég, / Sírnak a fellegek. / Álmaimban mindig haza járok, / Várnak reám akik szeretnek.—Above me weeps the sky / Sadly the dark clouds roam / Dreaming, I wing, I fly / My loved ones are waiting at home."

But no one was waiting.

By eight o'clock I had visited all the homes I remembered. Eyes smarting, hair dripping, clothes wet, I dragged myself back to our hotel. An outdoor stand offered sumptuous fresh peaches, and I stopped in the rain to buy some for our breakfast. Our young waiter was offended. "We have citrus juice for our foreign guests," he boasted. "Imported from America!"

Ilona chose fresh squeezed peach juice from the menu, but to please him, I tried the citrus. I was forced to spit it out: canned lemon juice—sour as vinegar. Tilting my chair on its hind legs, I shook with uncontrollable laughter. But then tears flowed, and I felt better. "I needed this," I told Ilona.

Leaving a generous tip, I got up from the table. A few minutes later, Ilona and I were calmly stepping along the glistening street, looking every bit the American tourists we were—with our Nike shoes, L. L. Bean clothes, and SLR camera. It had stopped raining, and the slanted rays of the sun gently stroked my arms.

The hotel clerk had bragged about "our newly decorated downtown," but I was aghast at peeling stucco, crumbling frieze, cracking doors. True, a few blocks were freshly painted, but the rest had been neglected for decades. The shop windows displayed a scant supply of shoddy merchandise, except the delicatessen. "Hungarians still eat well," Ilona remarked.

"And drink," I smiled, commenting on the fine choice of wines and liqueurs. "We'll try some great Tokay *aszu* tonight."

"Where do we go this morning?" Ilona asked. "What do we see?"

"We'll visit the old town, Ilona—a small stage, my childhood. No wonder I never developed a sense of direction."

"We'll forgive you, Mom."

The Catholic church still dominated Kaposvár's main square, despite a flag displaying the hammer and sickle on neighboring city hall. Keeping peace between the two, the fatherly statue of nineteenth-century patriot Lajos Kossuth guarded the main square still named for him.

Many streets had been renamed under the new regime, I noted, though most people still used the old designations. Red and yellow cannas flaunted their summer skirts as if nothing had happened since I left here.

Soon, we reached Castle Street with its familiar houses: the Winternitzes' low structure hugging their grocery; the more stately Pogány house facing it from across the street. "Both families perished during the war," I told Ilona, trying to sound matter-of-fact. "No survivors."

"Where did your friends die?"

"Nobody knows for sure. Böde Winternitz and Ági Salgó were probably gang-raped on the Russian front. Ilona Pogány, her sister Évi, and Zsuzsi Schwarzenberg escaped that fate; they caught scarlet fever and were gassed at Auschwitz. Évi Kárpáti was gassed too, at the last selection at Auschwitz. She looked skeletal, I've been told."

We entered the gate of the Pogány house, a slum tenement now, the garden choking with weeds. The spacious porch, where I had enjoyed so many gracious meals, held a rusty icebox, a broken baby carriage, and three overflowing garbage pails.

My eyes fled to the cobbled yard. Near the neglected grape arbor I glimpsed some camomile we used to gather to rinse Ilona's and Évi's silky blond hair. Slowly, I crushed some in my fingers. "Let's leave, Ilona," I shivered at the fragrance. "I spent too much time here this morning. I can't take it anymore."

Ilona and I walked on, snapping photographs. Our former home on Kontrássy Street had been turned into a spartan health club, our copper-colored stove forlorn in a corner. On a stark wall, above a row of metal lockers, a tin clock marked time.

My preparatory school, the girls' gimnazium of Kaposvár, now bore a sign: "Boarding School for Children of Railroad Employees." I rang the bell; the janitor let us in. Ilona and I took the wide steps two at a time, as I used to do. I hastened to Dr. Biczó's former study. "No books," I groaned at the bare walls and metal furnishings. "I wish I had never come back here."

Next we walked on to Berzsenyi Street. The once-proud synagogue bore a sign we did not heed: DANGEROUS TO APPROACH; it looked as if no one had been near it in decades. Ilona and I walked around the tall, neglected building, staring through broken stained-glass windows at the upheaval: lights smashed, benches uprooted, although this temple had never been bombed.

• • •

At last we set out for my Vágó grandparents' house at 45 Berzsenyi Street—our ghetto home. Ilona glanced at my gold locket. "Didn't this belong to your grandmother Vágó?"

"It was her watch," I nodded, "but the mechanism rusted away in the cellar cave.

"And your father's signet ring, the one he inherited from Papa Klein?"

"The baker Ulrich must have dug it up from under the rose bush. When Aunt Magda returned briefly after the war, she obtained a permit to search the premises but found none of our belongings, only the contents of the cellar cave. In it, an urn of rancid goose fat, a handful of

The abandoned Jewish temple of Kaposvár (1977). Behind Ilona, the note on the door warns: "Dangerous to approach." (See the broken windows and the peeling stucco.)

jewelry, some family papers and photographs. The Nazi Ulrich had taken everything else. After John's birth, I remembered my grandfather's ring, and I wrote to Aunt Ica's widowed husband—my only remaining Kaposvár relative—to buy it back for me. But Ulrich had died. On a trip to the countryside to buy flour, he was hit by lightning."

"Lightning! But you never told me!"

"I don't think I ever mentioned Ulrich to you."

• • •

The former Vágó establishment was hardly recognizable: stucco crumbling, roof caving in. A winsome Gypsy woman opened the gate: a plump baby sucking her breast, a grimy little girl peeking from behind her mother's flowery skirt that lazily swept the ground. "Come in, come in," the woman ushered us into the courtyard.

I looked around, my heart shamelessly pounding, but nothing seemed the same, only the spreading tree in the middle of the cobbled yard—lush and green, smiling with apricots. "My grandfather planted this tree," I murmured, fingertips stroking the gnarled trunk.

"No, Madam," the Gypsy mother corrected me softly, "it was *my* father who planted it. Your tree died when I was a child."

We got permission from the present dwellers to visit their one-room apartments, but few mementos remained. Grandmother Vágó's wood-fired cook stove mourned darkly in its corner, reminding me of wax beans with apricot jam, our last meal here.

"Let's go," I told Ilona, glad to make my escape. "I've got to meet a former classmate."

To my surprise, six former classmates waited for me at the Hotel Dorottya—all who still lived in the county of Somogy. I recognized Sári Móritz at once: bronze curls, impish nose, gymnastic figure. "All your best friends fled Kaposvár, Jutka," said Dr. Móritz, now a local physician, as she pulled up a chair next to mine. "None of Dr. Biczó's 'harem' remained here. By the way, Ági Toronyi, Baba Vertelényi and Márta Magay send their love; they're arranging a Budapest reunion for you. My mother wants to be remembered too," Sári added with a smile. "Remember the sea green gown she once lent you for a costume? She's still got it in the attic. You know, Mother always mentions you when she unpacks her old things."

Does anyone else?—I wondered.

"My mother and my aunt Magda send regards," I told my classmates, as I tasted the fragrant wild mushroom soup. "Mother made her home with us for several decades and ran a successful gift store in town. She hasn't remarried."

"And your aunt Magda?"

"Magda lost her husband during the war, but later she married another widowed survivor, Michael Vass, in America. They have a married son, Andrew, whom they adore. Just recently, Magda and her husband retired next door to my mother in Florida. How I wish I could take them some wild mushrooms."

Of course, my classmates and I exchanged family photographs, but mostly we spoke of the past: the tension before exams; the jokes, the pranks.

My gentile hosts seemed uncomfortable with the Holocaust and made only tentative remarks about our Jewish classmates who died: Évi Kárpáti, Ági Salgó, Agáta Schöber, and Böde Winternitz. Instead, the talk soon focused on Professor Biczó, and the legends that had multiplied. "You must visit his grave, Jutka," Sári told me, sipping her espresso. "We all do, regularly."

Erzsébet S. must have guessed my thoughts: "It's true, Jutka, I was no brain and never got any A's, but my kids think I'm a sage. And everything I know, I learned from Dr. Biczó."

After lunch, Ilona and I embarked on the three-kilometer climb to the cemetery. Sweaty and out of breath, we entered the familiar black iron gates of the Jewish graveyard. Ilona had heard about my grandfathers' funerals, but she was surprised to find the tombstones of remote ancestors as well—including my great-great-grandparents. "Dávid and Julianna Slovák," I deciphered the worn etching. "He lived to eighty-three and she to ninety-seven," I translated for Ilona, adding: "and without the aid of antibiotics."

"David and Julia," Ilona murmured. "They'd be fine names for kids."

"That's right," I smiled at my daughter.

"I never realized that your family had lived in Kaposvár for so long," she quickly changed the subject. "Five generations!"

Tibor L., the president of the Jewish community—consisting of some forty people instead of the more than three thousand I recalled, met us at the monument to the martyrs of World War I. The memorial was familiar to me from childhood, engraved with the names of fourteen men, two of them decorated heroes.

Next to it, Tibor pointed to a memorial I had never seen before: ten graceful columns surrounding an urn. "To the memory of the martyrs of World War II," I read.

My family. My friends. Moments of long ago flashed through my mind: if I hadn't defied the selection at Auschwitz, hadn't been pulled from the transport at Lichtenau, hadn't escaped the death march at Leipzig, the bombs, the guns, my name would be engraved on this monument, under my father's.

I inspected the columns, but found no names. "Tibor, where are the names of the victims?"

He shook his head: "We couldn't engrave them."

"Why not?"

"Too many names."

"How many?" I shuddered.

"Out of more than five thousand deported from our area, only some two hundred and fifty survived. Five percent."

I leaned against a column, suddenly dizzy.

"You are awfully pale," Ilona held me. "Sit down and rest."

• • •

Later, we said good-bye to Tibor and walked across the street to the Catholic cemetery. Following my classmates' instructions, we found Dr. Biczó's grave, an earthen mound strewn with smooth pebbles and wilted flowers. Reading the inscription on the black iron cross, Ilona remarked: "Dr. Biczó died in 1945, I see. Another war victim?"

"In a way, yes." Placing a smooth, round pebble among the rest, I straightened up with a sigh: "Let's get back to our hotel, Ilona. Enough cemeteries."

As we descended into the sunset, Ilona turned to me: "Tell me about Dr. Biczó. What happened to him?"

"A good man," I mused, "I used to think him one of the best. Do you know what Sári Móritz just told me? Dr. Biczó died of sorrow over his martyred students. Very melodramatic, isn't it? Unfortunately, there's another version. The night before last, a childhood acquaintance told me in Budapest that Dr. Biczó drank himself into the grave—haunted by a bad conscience."

"A bad conscience?"

"Apparently, soon after our transport left for Auschwitz, Dr. Biczó was called to military duty and placed in charge of a Jewish forced labor unit. His men were eventually transported to a German concentration camp, but after the war, a single survivor returned to Kaposvár. He claimed that Dr. Biczó had been a harsh Kommandant, cruel when drunk and frequently drunk."

"Do you believe that? It's hearsay from a single witness."

"With a survival rate of 5 percent, how can there be many witnesses? Dr. Biczó liked his wine, that much I know, and being in charge of a forced labor camp does harden a person."

"Suppose it's true about Dr. Biczó. Could you forgive him?"

"Had I stayed a kapo's helper at Auschwitz, could I forgive myself? You know, of all the things I lost during the war, I wish I had Plato's *Gorgias* still. Dr. Biczó had underlined a quote by Socrates in black ink: 'It is better to suffer an injustice than to commit one.' Perhaps this prompted me to quit assisting the kapo at Auschwitz."

"Where did Dr. Biczó die? In Kaposvár?"

"Yes, that much is clear. And everyone agrees that he was despondent in the summer of 1945. Most of his Jewish students had been killed; he must have mourned them. Then came the report about Marika Erdős—his all-time favorite. When he heard it, Dr. Biczó collapsed of a heart attack. My classmates insist that he died on Eszterházy Street, in front of the girls' gimnazium of Kaposvár."

"Marika Erdős? The girl who lent you her Hungarian costume? What happened to her?"

"Raped and killed."

"Was she Jewish?"

"According to the Nazis, she was—although her parents had converted before Marika was born. But she escaped Auschwitz. In the spring of 1944, Marika was attending the University of Budapest . . ."

"Budapest Jews weren't all taken," Ilona remembered. "The Russian invasion interfered, didn't it?"

"Yes, but Jewish girls were still being transported—directly to the Russian front. Marika escaped that ordeal as well: university friends hid her in an attic."

"Like Anne Frank."

"In a way, yes, but Marika was never discovered. The day the Russians liberated Budapest, Marika was among the first to venture into the streets. The capital was in tumult, drunken troops everywhere, hardly any women in sight. Marika was raped and shot on the bank of the Danube."

"Oh, no!"

We were climbing toward the peak now, panting hard; upper Main Street seemed steeper than when I used to coax my two-wheeler up by its handlebars. On the crest, we stopped to rest. A brick-red sun perched on the horizon, illuminating Kaposvár's rooftops, just as I remembered them.

I was still projecting Marika Erdős's image with the flowing brown hair and the full breasts I had envied, when Ilona softly said: "Thousands of women were raped during the war, but no one hears about them."

"The Anne Franks who survived rape don't write their stories."

"Will you?"

"I've already finished one chapter, Ilona. After this trip, I know I'll go on. I seem to owe it to the dead."

"You owe it the living," Ilona suggested.

My Letters to Maine, U.S.A.
Berneck-am-Fichtelgebirge • Fall 1945

MY LETTER TO IKE'S FATHER AND STEPMOTHER

This undated letter was sent to Popham Beach, Maine, soon after our engagement. (Please note original spelling.)

Dear Family,

Forgive Ike that he makes such a foolishness and marries me. I kno you much better, than you do me and I think we shall love each other very much. I ask always Ike, as a child for fairy tales, to tell me about you and Popham, so good is, after this year, to hear about a family and a home, which will be mine. The tales finish by Ike looking at me very carefully and seriously and saying: they will all love you very much. So, he promised it and I ought to believe him without doubt. I am quite ashamed to awaite your letter as nervously as I do. I was very accustomed to family life and your love is so much important to me.

Are you not very worried about this strange marriage and not too much affraid of this unknown Hungarian girl who expects father and mother in you?

Love,
Jutka

LETTER TO FRAN

This letter was found among my late father-in-law's papers after my manuscript had been completed.

Berneck, 11.9.1945

Dear Fran!

I wanted to write this letter in French, but I just wonder, that maybe I could write it in English too. I should like it so much, that I have to try it. I think, the worst which can happen, that you will laugh a lot about. And since I think, you like to laugh, so this is not so very bad neither. I just hope, you will understand the letter. Please, be cautious. Instead of "no," I often say "not" and instead of "stingy," I say "stinky" which is probably not the same, but very similar—for me. So, if I write something strange, you have to know, I didn't mean that.

I hope, you already got my answer written last week. I am even now so happy with your letter and with both dresses. I simply cannot tell how.

Ike is already gone for a journey of about ten days. I have now plenty of time and I try to write you the letter I wanted to write for such a long time. It was because of the difficulties of the language, I waited so long. I think, you must be interested of my past and also of the life of the Jews in German camps, and perhaps you don't want to ask me about because you think, it may disturb me. It is not disagreeable to me to tell about. I don't want to be strange or unkown to you.

Till my nineteenth year I was really a child and a very happy one. I was born in a little town of Hungary, Kaposvar. My father was an employer[1] and we had a very quiet and nice life at home. My parents were very young and we three were the best friends you can imagine. We were even a little too much devoted to each other, if one of us was a little ill, the two others were quite out of themselves. I think my par-

---

1. *Tisztviselő*—officeholder.

ents are quite wonderful people, I hope you will be able to know them. We had quite a great[2] family in Kaposvar. My four grandparents, my four young, unmarried friend-uncles and two lovely aunts with their husbands. I was the only child. So it is quite natural that they all loved me very much. My two grandfathers died at home, one before the first[3] Jewish law, the other just before our depart from Hungary. They were very fortunate. I am now with my mother and one of my aunts. The other was put into gas. My two grandmothers too. I don't know anithing about my uncles. Two disappeared three years ago on the Russian front. They were in Jewish working camps there. We left the others in the same kind of camps. My father too. I just happened to know, that my father was brought to Buchenwald and sent from there to some working camp. I believe very strongly, that he is just as alright as we are. Sometimes still I am very very anxious to know it sure and to see him already. It is very hard to wait so long. I hope, next month we shall be able to find out something about him.

I had a lot of friends at home, now naturally I don't know anything about them neither. We had a very happy time together. I liked to go to scool, where being a Hungarian gimnasium, we were thought many unuseful things. Such as Hungarian litterature, history, geography, history of art, Latin language, history, Litterature and high algerbra. I really don't know what for. The only practical things I know, this little English and French, I learned privately.[4] And I also learned German, especially grammatic, privat from my grandfather. From all other things I know poorly few and I wait very much some books from you to begin learning. The gimnazium was in all quite easy and I had plenty of time for sporting and reading. I naturally read mostly Hungarian, please don't laugh about that. Nobody believes me, but Hungarian litterature is good.

After the gimnasium I wanted to go to the University, first in Budapest, and after the war I wanted to go travel[5] a little in Europe. (not quite as I've done now). I was quite desolate sometimes that I know so little about life and people. Now I got it. I learned very much about both of them in quite a short time. Now I have no other desire but to have home and love and a quiet life again.

Still I cannot tell you, that I was very unhappy in the lagers.[6] The

2. Large family.
3. It should be: second Jewish Law.
4. I had eight years of German and four years of French in the gimnazium, but the classes were not conversational.
5. I did not specify to Ike's family my renounced dream, Paris and the Sorbonne.
6. Camps.

whole thing was so terrible that in some strange way it was more amusing than I could expect.

During the journey from Hungary to Auschwitz, in Poland we were all ready to die. We were 75 in one waggon, we could hardly sit and for three days we didn't get any water.[7] Some people grew mad. Some died. The waggon was closed, one couldn't put them out. Children were all quiet and brave like little heros. I am always affraid to ralise that all, all of them are dead. And their mothers too, because they didn't want to be separated from them. All Jewish children, young mothers, and old people almost from whole Europe.

We arrived in Auschwitz at night. Dead and mad people throne everywhere in the mud at the sideroad. In one minute we were separated to men and women standing by couples.[8] Then we were ordered to go forward and by a door of fence an SS dr was throing some of us to right some to left. I lost two grandmothers and an aunt of the same age as Anyu[9] (my mother). It was a miracle she remained with me. All women under 14[10] and over 38 ought to die. And most of them, almost all of them did. During the whole time we spent in lagers, we were told that this branch[11] was put in better lagers, with easy work, or no work at all and with better dwelling. There were some stories that the Germans want to exchange them for their prisoners of war. We heard only after liberation, that the entire group was put into gas. There were even some transports, which were put in gas entirely, without any selection. At times when Germans didn't need workers.

In Auschwitz the first night we were let into a bathehouse. When we cameout, we had to hold each other always by the hand with Anyu and Magda. We could so hardly recognise each other that when I first went a little away I searched my own mother on the same place for half an hour when I recognised her at last in the woman sitting there for all the time. We left everything, all our clothes, and even all our hair in the bathehouse. We came out in one dirty, old shirt and a terrible dress. The last ones without, covered with some grey blanket. Our heads were shaved quite bold. Without hair even in womenclothes,

---

7. Actually, we got a sip a day, but I did not know the word for "sip" in English.

8. By pairs.

9. Hungarian for Mama.

10. Should be under 16. I heard the SS say sixteen in Auschwitz, but I thought I had heard it wrong, because we had a fourteen year old and a fifteen year old with us in Lichtenau. As I found out later, they had given their age as sixteen in order to stay with their mother.

11. Group.

everybody looked man. For two days we couldn't get accostumed to it and we always told each other -please, Mr. or -hallo, my little boy.

We spent three weeks in Auschwitz, we got no water and from thirst we couldn't eat neither that very little bread we got. We had no place to lie down in the barracks being 500 in one room. We slept only for some minutes, sometimes sitting, sometimes even standing. We had to stand[12] outside from 3 in the morning till 7 in the evening. It was a terrible climate. In the morning we almost frose and at noontime I always had to think on stories about the Sahara. The sun shone terribly strong on our bold heads and we suffered from thirst more than from some very great pain.

This was July, after the beginning of the great invasion and at the time of the attack[13] against Hitler. We thought the war will be over in some days or by the worst case in some weeks. Sometimes when there was neither cold nor hot we were in quite natural mood. The women began to repair their dresses the first day. They borrowed the few pins they found in the dresses one from the other. They tore a piece of the long dresses and put it on the head to be nicer. Women are the strangest people I ever could immagine, and and the most interesting is that I am of the same sort. We were sewing, chattering, singing in this greatest powerty and desert of life anybody could imagine. I couldn't understand them if I were not the same. But even so, I often couldn't understand ourselves.

Once I was sitting in the dust in a terrible sunshine. Near me a bold, dirty, dryfaced, dumblooking creature. She looked as at home some mad beggar. I was just looking her poor face, when suddenly she turned to me and asked in the manner of the best society if I read the Brave new word from Huxley. And we began to speak about books.

We were the last transport, which arrived at Auschwitz and we were the first who left it.[14] We were separated in three groups. The weak and ill ones remained,[15] Anyu was put in the middle group, Magda and me in the strongest group. I came back three times to ask the SS dr to go with Anyu. The Polish woman told, he will kill me, but I didn't mind it too much then. At last they let me and Magda go with

12. Some days we stood in ranks from dawn to dusk, other days we were allowed to lie down on the ground.

13. The attempt made on Hitler's life by his own generals.

14. I meant from Lager B III.

15. It was only years later that I was able to confirm their fate: they had been killed as I had feared—gassed, actually.

Anyu. We were the only ones from three thousand who succeeded to insist the selection.

We came to Germany, to Lichtenau by Kassel. We worked in fields and in factories. We had very little time to sleep, very hard work to do and always less to eat. But most of the time we were in quite a good mood. When we were able to steal two potatoes, we were happy. The woods we went across at midnight in high snow were wonderful and sometimes we went across such pretty old little towns going to field work, they looked like Grimmtale illustrations. When for half an hour something was "caput" in the factory and we couldn't work, the whole branch of young girls I worked with, began to sing and dance. Once an SS girl saw me dancing a night and wanted to let cut my one inch long, new hair, but next evening I collapsed from weakness just before starting to go to work, I could remain at home and she forgot about me. Next night I probably danced again. We were packing shells of 36 pounds, one person 1000–3000 one night. I had a friend with me who was whistling Beethoven and Mozart quite well, I knew many poems, another was singing, the forth knew a lot of funny stories, we were in such good mood, the german "Forarbeiterin"[16] girls just stared at us and couldn't understand. In the last weeks we were so hungry that our whole amusement shortened to tell eachother what kind of soups and meats and vegetables and cakes our mothers used to make. Nobody of us knows exactly how to make, but we found out and explained very seriously. I learned to cook at nights in the factory. The real hunger began toward spring. At Sylvester night (31/12) for example we had still a big party. We lived 40–42 in room. It was a like a family. We knew each others good and bad habits and liked each other with all of them. Even now I think of our "room" as on a second family I lost. At Sylvester every room made a great party. We had wonderful sandwiches and pies[17] from black bread, potatoes, white cheese,[18] carrots, some margerine, few marmelade, some white carrots.[19] The long table was covered with white papers, nicely arranged sandwiches and paperdishes,[20] two green bottles of "Erzatz coffee" and the pies. We all cleaned our only cloth[21] and made a possibly "womanhair" for the great occasion. We sat around the table, which really looked like a

16. Female foreman.
17. Tiny pieces of bread cut in the round.
18. Cottage cheese.
19. Turnips.
20. Scraps of paper.
21. A singular for clothes. I meant: our only dress.

Sylvester table at home, and were very proud of it. Some girls had no place by the table, they sat on the top of the two storied beds, their legs hanging in the air, the lips red from colored pencil we had stolen from the factory. It was a good party with all the fun which is custom at a Sylvester night.

We looked already civilised then. The secret of that was our "market," where we could buy thread and pin, soap and comb, washpulver and shawl for one to five slices of bread. The sellers were Russian girls. Naturally the whole marketing was strictly forbidden. So the market-place was the W.C. There was always a crowd of Russian girls showing their wares and of Jewish with their very thin slices of bread. The Jewish girls tried to speak with words and gestures, to bargain, to ask, the Russian girls just smiled and they gave or didn't for the prise. One never knew if they understood our words or didn't. One could hear from everywhere—Ich, dir, geben, zwei, verstanden? zwei Brot. Du - mir - geben - Zwirne. Gut? Ich dir geben. . . . Du mir geben . . .[22] And the Russians just stood and smiled. All in a dirty little W.C. behind the factory.

The marketing had a quick finish when hunger began. Food was so terribly few the last months and especially the last weeeks, I always admired I still don't hear the bones clacking, when the poor hungry women, with their too modern waists and too uncertain steps, sadly climbed the road upstairs[23] to the factory.

In the last days I escaped every day from our resting-house and I spent whole my pause[24] digging with my fingers the dirthills of the factory kitchen. And I was happy when I could bring one half-ruined carrot home to Anyu, who was already ill from hunger then. But we were all the three very proud and happy, when I found sometimes four or five pieces. I only percieved what am I doing, when once a German woman went by and I saw her look. It was before the end of the war and she was probably afraid to suffer the same hunger in the future. It was funny. I looked at her very seriously and told very gently -Ich bin hungrig.[25] She run away like mad.

One night we heard the sound of canons from very far. The front came closer and we were listening at it happily for ten days. 5 hours before the Americans arrived to Lichtenau, we were transported away.

22. "I give you . . . understand? . . . two bread. You give me thread. Good? I give you. . . . You give me . . ."
23. Uphill.
24. Rest-period.
25. I am hungry.

We were travelling for 6 days, 100 women in one closed waggon. We could hardly move our feet and we didn't get to eat. The train was standing most of the time and we were sometimes wondering if they let us die inside. But some women were still stricking nice new stockings[26] and some were sewing, though there was no place to move hands. I was sewing too. A big pocket on my dress. It could become very useful for stolen potatoes or carrots anywhere we could arrive.

The sixth day we arrived to Leipzig. We were put in a lager, got a soup with two pieces of unpeeled potatoes and were perfectly happy. Next day some bombs fell on us. The whole lager burned away. We had four deads. We were put in another lager. 500 women in one room. During bombardment we were closed inside. There was no possibility to escape from fire or under ruines. We could see from the windows the bombardments of Leipzig, three, four, five times a day. The aeroplans covered the whole sky, the bombs fell like icerain and big fires burned in all directions. We were beside a big factory with munition. We were lying on the ground of the barrack, waiting for the bombs. Without fear, without any sound. Most girls were already quite strong[27] then. I was quite astonished that my hearth beated just as quiet as otherwise.

Americans came nearer again. When they reached the side of the city, we had to go away. Half an hour before starting we had quite a great idea, Anyu, Magda and me. We result to remain. The doctoress allowed to hide us in the ill-room. From 500 women nine remained there, six ill ones and we three. The transport went away, we were waiting for the Americans. Instead arrived 250 sick prisoners[28] from all nationality, they were put in our barrack. We were all waiting for the Americans. Suddenly came two SS girls, brought us nine to a woman lager. We ought to go with a transport of all kind of concentration prisoners.[29] We hid us all nine in the Hospital[30] again. The transport went away. Through the window we saw our last lager burning with the ill men inside. Three escaped to us trembling, half burned. An SS officer burned them. He came to our lager too, searching for Jewish women and the men who probably escaped here. The Polish and French[31]

---

26. A privileged few, Mrs. Dános and Mrs. Jámbor for instance, had been employed to knit stockings for the SS.

27. Emotionally, I meant.

28. Male prisoners of war.

29. Forced laborers.

30. Our temporary infirmary in the cellar.

31. To this day, I don't know whether the women who spoke French most fluently were French or Polish.

women denied us. We were in a separate room in the cellar, beside the half-burned men. No Polish or French woman dared to enter our room. We waited the SS man coming.[32] We waited every moment, he comes and finds us. We got plenty of food then. Sometimes I was happy, that even if I have to die now, before dying once I can eat enough. Sometimes I wondered that perhaps I am already dead and this is the paradise. When the Americans arrived, I was so full, I couldn't eat the chocolat, we dreamed so much about at night, in the factory.

It was very soon after our liberation that I made the aknoledge to Ike and Fred. After all, this was the most interesting thing which happened to me since I left home. Ike probably wants to tell himself about, so I leave it for him. Just wait some months or years and you'll know all about it, I am sure.

I never believed in fate or wonders. But I often think now, that I had to come to Auschwitz and Lichtenau, and I had to remain in Leipzig with the ill women and I had to go all these things through, only to meet Ike. We met ourselves quite by accident. But as I was too occupied with my own troubles to pay any attention to him, so by another accident we met ourselves after a week again. You know him so you can understand, how phantastic it is that I met just him in Leipzig, after so many chances, before going home. If I wasn't so accustomed to unusual things to happen, I couldn't believe, it's sure.

The only thing I was a little scared about, that now I go so far from my own family and maybe you will not recieve me as I need it. It is true, I have one uncle in America, the eldest brother of my father. But he is a professor at a college in New York which will be also far enough. When I got the letters of the family I had to laugh, how fortunate I am.

Dear Fran, if the other members of the family are also interested in me, please, show them this letter. As, instead of French, I wrote it in English, it is written to them equally.

Please, don't forget to send me photos about all the family. I am waiting very much.

Love to all,
Jutka

32. Returning.

Sources and Acknowledgments

My trip to Hungary was prompted by my desire to revisit the places I was describing, and my need for books and articles on the Hungarian Holocaust, but I did not know how to begin the research there.

My uncertainty was soon alleviated by my former friend and neighbor, Péter Hanák, who came to see us on arrival. Dr. Hanák had become an internationally known historian at the University of Budapest. Through Péter and his colleagues, I was soon able to locate the most important literature on the Hungarian Holocaust. Some of the works they recommended confirmed my memories and placed them into a historical context, others inspired my writing.

Eventually I was able to obtain the most important publications from university libraries in America:

Fekete Könyv (Black Book) by Lévai Jenő, available in English translation, *Black Book on the Martyrdom of Hungarian Jewry* by Eugene Lévai (The Central European Times Publishing Co. Ltd. Zurich, in conjunction with the Panorama Publishing Co. Ltd. Vienna, 1948).

This is the most detailed study of the various acts, laws, and events relating to the Holocaust in Hungary. With the help of the three volumes of the *Black Book* I was able to obtain dates, background information, and accurate data for events too numerous to mention.

A companion copy, the *Fehér Könyv (White Book)* by Lévai Jenő (published by Officiana, Budapest, 1946), helped me double-check important dates relating to the persecution of Hungarian Jewry in my story. The rest of the book deals with political events, which I found interesting but not very useful.

The third of the series was inspiring, but not particularily informative, because it deals mostly with excerpts from survivors' reports and poems: *Sárga Könyv, Adatok a Magyar Zsidóság Háborús Szenvedéseiből, 1941-1945 (Yellow Book, Facts of the Wartime Sufferings of Hungarian Jewry)* by Béla Vihar (published by Igazság Nyomda, Budapest [date not visible]).

Another work proved particularly helpful to me in describing the various prohibitions and "Jewish Laws" (or "Jewish bills") and their dates of appearance: *Vádirat a Nácizmus Ellen,* Dokumentumok a magyarországi zsidóültözés történetéhez. Két kötet. *(Indictment on Nazism*—Documents [relating] to the History of Jewish Persecutions, books I and II), by Ilona Beneschofsky and Elek Karsai (published by A Magyar Izraeliták Országos Képviselet [The Hungarian Jews' National Representation] Budapest, 1958).

Before leaving Budapest for Kaposvár, I met with a dozen Jewish women who had moved from our hometown to the capital. We exchanged memories of our ghetto existence, but none were able to provide the information I lacked; we all recalled the events themselves, but not the order of their occurrence.

In Kaposvár, I was fortunate once again. I located a former teacher of mine, Béla Kellner, who, to my surprise, had served as head librarian of my home county of Somogy before his retirement that year. Mr. Kellner—whose younger brother had been hanged in Auschwitz for conspiracy—was most supportive of my writing. He offered to obtain all the information about Kaposvár I needed. Of course, Mr. Kellner had access to library files, including those closed to the general public, and he had excellent relations with city and county governmental agencies. He also knew the Jewish survivors of Kaposvár personally. All this proved immensely helpful to my research. I visited him the following summer, and I have been in active correspondence with him ever since.

Mr. Kellner eventually combed through the local newpaper editions of the period and mailed all the microfilmed articles that dealt with the Holocaust in the *Somogy Napló,* the local paper. (I shall never forget the evening when I, the former dean, sat down before a modern screen in a solitary corner of the elegant Bates College library and read those decades-old news articles on the ghetto of my hometown.) With the help of the *Black Book* and the microfilmed articles, I was able to reconstruct an accurate chronicle of the crowded events of April to July 1944.

Mr. Kellner reads English well, and he recently proofread my manuscript for accuracy. He checked all the details against the official papers and the memories of former comrades. (I must say that he made few corrections; my memory and research served me well.)

In July 1978, I revisited Auschwitz with my son, John Magyar Isaacson, and his wife. We spent a day inspecting the place, and I was able to get some specific information.

Most important, I found out why some of my own recollections differed from the accounts I had read. Our transport was among the last ones to come from Hungary on July 8, 1944, and due to the unusual number of arrivals, the SS were forced to change their customary procedures. The gas chambers and crematoria couldn't accommodate everyone judged unfit for work, so hundreds were piled along the railroad tracks to be immolated—just as I had feared.

It was due to this heartless haste that we were housed in half-finished barracks, clothed in rags, marked with a painted red cross instead of wearing prisoners' garb, and provided with hardly any food or water. It was also due to this haste that we escaped tattooing.

While visiting the Auschwitz museum, John asked our young Polish guide to tell us something about Birkenau, Lager B III. This prompted a memorized paragraph she uttered in a Polish lilt:

"Lager B III used to be called 'Mexico' by the other inmates. It was the poorest of the poor. No food, no water. No one survived there for more than three weeks."

John said softly, as he glanced at me: "This is my mother. In the summer of 1944, she spent three weeks in Lager B III."

Mutely, the young girl stared at me as if I were some ghost. At last she muttered, shaking her head: "I don't know right words. Pleased to meet you."

"Pleased to be alive," I nodded.

In Auschwitz, I had a chance to relive some of my memories. We found the puddle near the foundation of our former barrack, where my friend Ilona Pogány and I had so calmly discussed suicide. The wooden barrack had been burned down, and the electric wire fence was gone, but we located its torn remnants some fifty feet from the kidney-shaped puddle.

Today, Auschwitz is treated as a memorial to the Polish underground, and hardly any mention is made of the millions of Jews killed there. Only when I told our guide that we were Jewish did she obtain the keys to the Jewish museum.

John thought the exhibits most informative, and I did too, but I made the mistake of trying to identify my family and friends on too many gruesome films and photographs. Halfway through, I gasped, suddenly faint: "I must get some fresh air!"

"Sorry," our guide said pityingly. "The entrance is locked. One must go through to the end; that's how the museum was built."

At the museum I bought several books which proved helpful: *Auschwitz—Múzeumi Kalauz*—[museum guide] Az Auschwitz Muzeum Kiadványa (published by the Auschwitz Museum in 1976). This is a short but excellent account written in Hungarian. It contains some remarkably accurate maps, descriptions, and photographs of the Hun-

Auschwitz-Birkenau (1978). John helped me find the kidney-shaped puddle now overgrown with weeds. Note the row of cement blocks on the right, all that remained of our former barrack.

garian Jews in Auschwitz. There are whole pages depicting the life we led, and various photographs that brought back memories.

The most shocking books I bought there are in French:

Auschwitz Vu Par les S.S. by Höss, Broad, Kremer (Edition du Musée d'Etat à Oświęcim, 1974). It contains the journals of SS officers who describe Auschwitz in a cool and detached manner.

L'histoire du Kl Auschwitz, by Chech, Makowski, Mikulski, and Fiderkiewicz (Edition du Musée d'Etat à Oświęcim, 1978), has heartbreaking medical reports on the experiments conducted at Auschwitz.

Problèmes Choisis de l'Histoire du KL Auschwitz by Kazimierz Smolen, translated into French by Anna Novak-Bednarczyk (Edition du Musée d'Etat à Oświęcim, 1978). This edition is filled with significant and gory photographs which always remind me of walking through the Jewish museum at Auschwitz or Yad Vashem, the Holocaust museum in Jerusalem.

In 1981, I benefited by an oustanding study published in the U.S. that year: *The Politics of Genocide—The Holocaust in Hungary, Books I and II,* by Randolph L. Braham (New York: Columbia University Press, 1981). These exceptionally well written and detailed volumes provided me with important facts on the Jewish male forced labor camps, an area where my knowledge is secondhand, and clarified my recollections of other topics. One volume even contains a brief report on the ghetto in my hometown, Kaposvár—on pages 667–68—but regrettably misspells the name of its main street. It was *Berzsenyi* ucca, not *Berzsényi*. (The communist regime changed its name since to celebrate one of their more recent heroes.)

A friend of Hungarian origin, Dr. Éva S. Balogh of Connecticut, former instructor of Central European history at Yale University, checked my manuscript for relevant historical details and made countless insightful suggestions. In addition, she made available to me some of her exceptional collection of scholarly books on Hungary, among them the following:

Magyar történelmi kronológia (Hungarian historical chronology), edited by Péter Gunst (Budapest: Tankönyvkiadó, 1968).

Her rare volume of *Magyar zsidó lexikon-* (Hungarian Jewish Lexicon), edited by Péter Ujváry (Budapest: Magyar zsidó lexicon, 1929).

I benefited especially by Eva Balogh's most recent article: "Hungarian Foreign Policy, 1918–1945" in *The Hungarians: A Divided Nation,* edited by Stephen Borsody (New Haven: Yale Center for International and Areas Studies, 1988).

Of course, I read many general studies on the Holocaust, but I never saw any reference made to our camp in Hessisch Lichtenau, nor did I expect to find any. My husband and I journeyed there in 1983, hoping to obtain information for my book, but our visit proved disappointing. We managed to locate a few factory buildings and the site of our former barracks, but we gathered no oral history and received no sympathy from the inhabitants. Until quite recently, my chapters on Hessisch Lichtenau lacked verification.

Then, through a former comrade, Éva (Jámbor) Baik of Budapest, a book appeared on my desk quite unexpectedly in January 1987, written specifically about us, the one thousand Hungarian Jewish women who had slaved in Lichtenau: *Das Aussenkommando Hessisch Lichtenau des Konzentrationslagers Buchenwald, 1944/45*, by Dieter Vaupel, published in 1984 by Gesamthochschule Kassel, Fachbereiche 1 und 5.[1]

This scholarly study by a local history teacher—who had since become a university professor—turned up documents I never dreamt existed. For instance, on pages 84–87, it shows the official paper on the group of two hundred and six volunteers who were actually sent back to Auschwitz. My mother, my aunt Magda, and I would have been part of that group, had the kapo, Manci Pál, failed to pull us out.

Mr. Vaupel's book provided hard data I had lacked, and it eventually led me back to Hessisch Lichtenau for a third time, in September 1987. Through the efforts of a group of dedicated young Germans, led by Dieter Vaupel, Gisela Höfert, and Jürgen Jessen, a reunion was staged for us survivors, with all expenses paid by German authorities, including airfare.

Over forty of the original one thousand attended: Dr. Luciana Nissim, the former head of our infirmary, from Italy, Maida Pollock (Meda Dános) and I from the U.S., some thirty women from Hungary, and about a dozen from Israel. (No one knows how many of us survived the war, nor how many are still living.) We spent five days in Hessisch Lichtenau, and paid an emotional visit to the site of our former factory in Fürstenhagen, an area now renamed Hirschhagen. The reunion provided me with significant oral history to strengthen my chapters on Lichtenau.

I also discovered from Mr. Vaupel that our workplace by Fürstenhagen happened to be one of the three largest munitions factories in Germany, which employed as many as eight thousand forced laborers. It seems that I, who have always been affiliated with small cities and smaller schools, had the dubious privilege of having been enslaved

1. Postsecondary Educational Institute Kassel, Departments 1 and 5.

At our former workplace (September 1987). Maida Pollock (formerly Meda Dános) reminisces by the tracks where she used to unload shells off my hand-pulled wagon.

Reunion at Hessisch Lichtenau (September 1987). I stand with some of my former comrades—the fourth from the left.

by two of Europe's most gigantic institutions—Dynamit Nobel and Auschwitz.

Quite independently from Mr. Vaupel's efforts, another scholar had been involved with our fate for decades: Benjamin B. Ferencz, lawyer, professor, and well-known author, a onetime American prosecutor at Nürnberg and the director of the restitution efforts on behalf of Jewish survivor groups. Through Dr. Ferencz's efforts, we survivors of the original one thousand who could be still located received a modest restitution in the summer of 1987.

In his excellent book *Less than Slaves* (Harvard University Press, 1979), Dr. Ferencz describes his legal battles to obtain restitution for the former slaves of Hitler's regime. On page 159, there is a paragraph about the one thousand of us who were sent from Auschwitz to Hessisch Lichtenau to labor in the munitions factory in nearby Fürstenhagen. Our company was called "Fabric Hessisch-Lichtenau der GmbH zur Verwertung chemische Erzeugnisse, a subsidiary of Dynamit Nobel." We were attached to Buchenwald, it seems, just as Mr. Vaupel learned quite independently. It does explain why our locked cattle car idled so long at the Weimar-Buchenwald railroad station before Buchenwald was liberated and we proceeded to Leipzig.

Dieter Vaupel, who has written a book about our group since our liberation, sent me a photograph of our Lichtenau barracks and a copy of the original SS document which lists our one thousand names, complete with the numbers assigned to us.

All the photos and documents stem from our family's personal collection unless otherwise noted. Photos dating before July 1944 survived in the cave I had dug in my grandparents' root cellar; those dating after 1977 were taken on my return trips to Hungary, Poland, and Germany.

In writing my memoirs, I have been extremely fortunate to have had the assistance of my mother, Rose Vágó Magyar and my aunt, Magda Vágó Vass (formerly Rosenberger), both of Deerfield Beach, Florida, who checked my memoir from beginning to end for accuracy, often rekindling my memory.

Two more former comrades examined my manuscript in detail: Éva (Jámbor) Baik of Budapest and Maida (Dános) Pollock of Princeton, N.J.—both fluent in English. I also had the advice of two psychiatrists, Dr. Maria Feder of Geneva—who had shared my Auschwitz and Lichtenau experiences—and Dr. Stephen Ring of Philadelphia—whose childhood in Kaposvár paralleled mine. These witnesses, to whom I am indebted, found my memory accurate; I had forced myself to evoke the past by virtual self-hypnosis, until whole conversations popped out in Hungarian—a tongue I hadn't used in decades.

Special thanks are due to Ms. Penelope Laurens, editor-in-chief of *The Yale Review,* who was instrumental in the acceptance of my excerpt on Auschwitz in the Spring 1984 issue of the magazine.

I was extremely fortunate to have the advice and support of my literary agent, Julian Bach of New York.

I am deeply indebted to friends who steered my book toward publication, and to Judith McCulloh, executive editor of the University of Illinois Press, who directed its acceptance with care and insight. I want to thank the many people who worked so hard on the book, especially Patricia Hollahan, manuscript editor, who took such a personal interest in every detail.

I am most deeply indebted to my three "pre-editors" who have been assisting me all these years. My daughter, Ilona Isaacson Bell, an associate professor of English at Williams College, and her husband, Robert Huntley Bell, professor of English at Williams College, gave me advice, encouragement, and instruction throughout, which proved essential for the writing. A talented Bates student, Daniel Griffin, who is now publications editor for Harvard University, volunteered his considerable expertise from start to finish. From Dan, Bob, and Ilona I learned to edit my own work and to "cut and paste"—mostly cut—a task which became less painful thanks to my Macintosh computer.

My sister-in-law, Shirley Isaacson Nadel of Israel, assisted me with the research at Yad Vashem.

My husband, Irving Isaacson, authenticated my chapters on Leipzig and checked facts and dates against his memorabilia of 1945: his OSS documents, his officer's diary, and his letters home. In 1983, Ike participated in the most thrilling part of my research, locating the house in Berneck-am-Fichtelgebirge where we got engaged. His constant and cheerful support has been essential for my decade-long sustained effort.

Index